About This Book

Why is this topic important?

Trainers know that learners understand concepts and acquire skills faster when they participate in their own learning. Case studies are a great training method to increase participation, make learning more enjoyable, and enhance retention of knowledge and skills as well as influence learners' attitudes. So why aren't case studies used more often in training? One reason is that many trainers find it difficult to write a realistic case study that meets a clearly defined learning objective without identifying the "guilty" parties in one's own organization.

What can you achieve with this book?

With this book, you will quickly and easily learn how to adapt a case study for your situation and how to create an original case study. To get the most out of each case study, facilitator notes are provided with a learning objective, answers to each case study, and facilitator processing or debriefing questions and suggested answers.

How is this book organized?

The first part of this book defines the five types of case studies and their different purposes. The benefits of using case studies along with cautions are included. Suggestions are provided for how to write an original case study or customize an existing case study. Steps for facilitating case studies for the greatest learning are outlined along with suggested processing or debriefing questions.

Part 2 contains twelve chapters for different training topics. If you are familiar with using case studies and are looking for a case study on a particular topic, you can easily locate the topic and case study using both the table of contents and index in the book.

All of the case studies in the second half of this book are on the enclosed CD-ROM (CD) and can be used as is, or modified to meet specific learning objectives.

About Pfeiffer

Pfeiffer serves the professional development and hands-on resource needs of training and human resource practitioners and gives them products to do their jobs better. We deliver proven ideas and solutions from experts in HR development and HR management, and we offer effective and customizable tools to improve workplace performance. From novice to seasoned professional, Pfeiffer is the source you can trust to make yourself and your organization more successful.

Essential Knowledge Pfeiffer produces insightful, practical, and comprehensive materials on topics that matter the most to training and HR professionals. Our Essential Knowledge resources translate the expertise of seasoned professionals into practical, how-to guidance on critical workplace issues and problems. These resources are supported by case studies, worksheets, and job aids and are frequently supplemented with CD-ROMs, websites, and other means of making the content easier to read, understand, and use.

Essential Tools Pfeiffer's Essential Tools resources save time and expense by offering proven, ready-to-use materials—including exercises, activities, games, instruments, and assessments—for use during a training or team-learning event. These resources are frequently offered in loose-leaf or CD-ROM format to facilitate copying and customization of the material.

Pfeiffer also recognizes the remarkable power of new technologies in expanding the reach and effectiveness of training. While e-hype has often created whizbang solutions in search of a problem, we are dedicated to bringing convenience and enhancements to proven training solutions. All our e-tools comply with rigorous functionality standards. The most appropriate technology wrapped around essential content yields the perfect solution for today's on-the-go trainers and human resource professionals.

Essential resources for training and HR professionals

Instant Case Studies: How to Design, Adapt, and Use Case Studies in Training

Instant Case Studies: How to Design Adapt, and Use Case Studies in Training

JEAN BARBAZETTE

Published by Pfeiffer
An Imprint of Wiley.
989 Market Street, San Francisco, CA 94103-1741 www.pfeiffer.com

For additional copies/bulk purchases of this book in the U.S. please contact 800-274-4434.
Pfeiffer books and products are available through most bookstores. To contact Pfeiffer directly call our Customer Care Department within the U.S. at 800-274-4434, outside the U.S. at 317-572-3985, fax 317-572-4002, or visit www.pfeiffer.com.

Pfeiffer also publishes its books in a variety of electronic formats. Some content that appears in print may not be available in electronic books.

ISBN: 0-7879-6885-4

Library of Congress Cataloging-in-Publication Data

Barbazette, Jean, 1943–
Instant case studies for successful training: how to design, adapt, and use case studies in training/ Jean Barbazette.
p. cm.
Includes bibliographical references and index.
ISBN 0–7879–6885–4 (alk. paper)
1. Case method—Handbooks, manuals, etc. 2. Training—Handbooks, manuals, etc.
3. Employees—Training of—Handbooks, manuals, etc. I. Title.
LB1029.C37B37 2004
658.3'124—dc22 2003016270

Acquiring Editor: *Matthew Davis*
Director of Development: *Kathleen Dolan Davies*
Editor: *Lupe Ortiz*
Production Editor: *Michael Bohrer-Clancy*
Manufacturing Supervisor: *Bill Matherly*
Editorial Assistant: *Laura Reizman*
Interior Design: *Gene Crofts*
Cover Design: *Bruce Lundquist*
Printed in the United States of America
Printing 10 9 8 7 6 5 4 3 2 1

To my children,

CHRISTOPHER and LESLIE,

who have enriched our lives.

ACKNOWLEDGMENTS

Special thanks to:

- Richard, my husband, who is a wonderful source of ideas
- Linda Ernst, my friend and Senior Instructor for The Training Clinic, for her targeted and timely suggestions
- Matthew Davis, my editor, who believed in my idea for this book
- Kelly Barbazette, my daughter-in-law, who created the index and gave editing assistance

CONTENTS

PART 2

Case Study Exercises

Each chapter in Part 2 offers five types of case studies for twelve workshops available on CD. Suggestions to use each case study are given, including discussion questions and suggested answers to case study questions. Facilitator processing questions and suggested answers to facilitator processing questions help you use these 71 cases instantly.

Case Study Topics by Chapter Number

LIST OF CASE STUDIES

Key Terms for Five Types of Case Studies

1. **Identification case study:** This type of case study helps learners identify both positive and negative characteristics of a situation.
2. **Problem-solving case study:** This type of case study helps the learner use systematic and creative problem-solving techniques.
3. **Practice case study:** This type of case study helps learners think about and use a new idea or try out a skill in a safe setting before using it in the real world.
4. **Application case study:** This type of case study is often used at the end of a training program to summarize and review a set of complex ideas and skills presented during the course.
5. **Serial case study:** This type of case study uses an initial situation or set of characters and progressively adds new elements for the learner's consideration.

List of Case Studies by Title

These are the case studies that appear on the CD. Throughout the book, the case studies are numbered and appear in the following order on the CD. This CD icon appears in the margin along with the number of each case study to identify which case study to find on the CD.

INTRODUCTION

Purpose

Instant Case Studies will help learners discover the concepts you are trying to teach. When key concepts are discovered as part of a training program, learners more readily embrace them. The end result of using case studies is to provide a note of reality, speed the rate of learning, and make learning more enjoyable. The 71 case studies in this book can be used instantly or adapted to meet your situation.

Audience

This book is intended for trainers who work in physical classrooms, virtual classrooms, or occasionally train others on the job. Trainers in any sector of business, non-profit or government organizations can instantly use the case studies as a part of any training program.

Product Description

Instant Case Studies is divided into two parts and includes a CD. The first part of the book contains three chapters describing:

1. The purpose and types of case studies
2. How to write and customize a case study
3. How to facilitate a case study

The second part of *Instant Case Studies* contains twelve chapters on a variety of training topics. Each chapter contains up to five different types of case studies with participant discussion questions. Following each case study, "Facilitator Notes" provide a learning objective for the case study, suggested answers to participant discussion questions, and facilitator processing questions to debrief the case study discussion along with suggested answers to the facilitator processing questions.

The CD contains 71 case studies and participant discussion questions that may be reprinted and/or customized using the permission guidelines in the front of this book. Each case study is numbered and provided in a Word file. A list of case studies by number and title is included.

Explanation of the Five-Step Adult Learning Model

How to facilitate a discussion of a case study is described in chapter 3. Briefly, the five-step adult learning model is used to ensure complete learning and retention. The five-step adult learning model is similar to other experiential learning models.

1. Set up the learning activity in which you will use the case study. Include the purpose of using a case study, what the case study is about, and how participants will organize themselves. Usually, individual preparation of discussion questions is followed by a small group discussion, then a debriefing occurs in a larger group using facilitator processing questions.

2. Participants read the case study, prepare answers, and discuss their answers in a small group.
3. A reporter from each group shares interpretations and reactions to the content of the case study by summarizing their answers to the discussion questions. Facilitator processing questions can be asked about how easy or difficult it was to discuss the issues raised in the case.
4. Additional facilitator processing questions ask the learners to develop the concept learned from the ideas or skills used in the case.
5. Participants are asked to plan how to apply what has been learned from the case to their own situation.

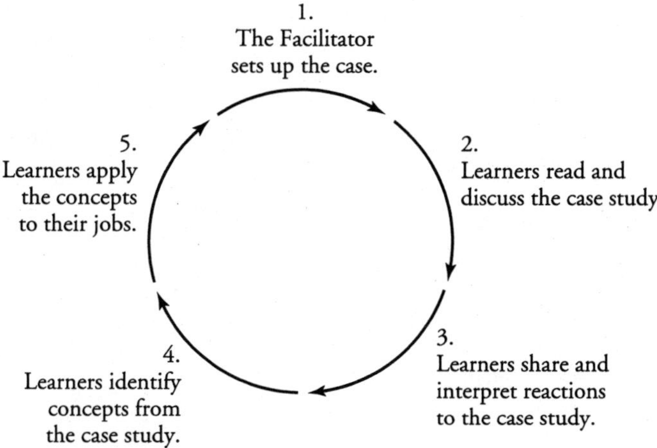
1.
The Facilitator sets up the case.
2.
Learners read and discuss the case study.
3.
Learners share and interpret reactions to the case study.
4.
Learners identify concepts from the case study.
5.
Learners apply the concepts to their jobs.

PART 1

Introduction to Part 1: Develop, Adapt, and Use Case Studies

To develop, adapt, and use case studies, chapter 1 of this book answers several questions about what a case study is, the benefits and cautions of using cases, and introduces five types of case studies. Each of the five types of case studies has a different purpose.

Chapter 2 suggests where case study development fits into the instructional design process, how to use an eight-step process to write an original case study, or how to adapt an existing case. Solutions to writing case studies are offered along with a series of templates to make writing and adapting case studies easy. Typical discussion questions are offered for learners and facilitators.

Chapter 3 offers suggestions to facilitate case study discussions using a five-step adult learning process to ensure the transfer of learning to the workplace.

WHAT'S IN THIS CHAPTER?

After reading this chapter, you will know:

What is a case study?

Why use five types of case studies?

What are the benefits of using case studies in training?

What are cautions when developing case studies?

How to recognize examples of the five types of case studies: identification, problem solving, practice, application, and serial.

1

Case Study Uses and Benefits

What Is a Case Study?

A case study is a description of an actual or made-up situation, which the learner examines to increase his or her knowledge and skills or to influence his or her attitudes. A case study is chosen by the trainer to present issues similar to the issues the learners are likely to encounter when trying to apply new knowledge and skills following a training program. A case study may be a paragraph, a page, or several pages. The amount of detail provided depends on the purpose of the case. A case study brings an element of realism to help the learner identify how to use and apply knowledge and skills. Case studies provide practice in diagnosing and solving problems and give ways to apply newly learned knowledge and practice skills.

Why Use Case Studies?

Typically, case studies are written for one of five purposes. These types of case studies are

1. **Identification:** This type of case study is appropriate to help learners identify both positive and negative characteristics of a situation.

As part of the learning process, the learner is asked to find points similar to those which may be present in his or her own work life. These provide a safer way to identify the characteristics or points from the case that they find in themselves.

2. **Problem Solving:** This type of case study helps the learner use systematic and creative problem solving techniques. Problem-solving case studies can be used to have learners solve an entire problem using a specific problem-solving model or to have learners focus on any part of the problem-solving process, such as finding a solution, or clearly identifying the problem.
3. **Practice:** This type of case study helps learners think about and use a new idea or try out a skill in a safe setting before using it in the real world. These case studies can also be used to help learners explore and clarify their attitudes about specific issues.
4. **Application:** This type of case study is often used at the end of a training program to summarize and review a set of complex ideas and skills presented during the course. Different elements of the case can address how the complex ideas that were learned are interrelated as well as show how to overcome obstacles to using new ideas and skills back on the job.
5. **Serial:** This type of case study uses an initial situation or set of characters and progressively adds new elements for the learner's consideration. Some of the elements from the above four types of cases may be used at different times during the workshop. This type of case study can save time since learners already understand the background of the case and can focus on the new element, idea, or skill being introduced. Another type of serial case study uses the same situation and asks the learners to use different tools and skills to apply to the same case study.

What Are the Benefits of Using Case Studies?

Case studies are often used in a training setting to add a note of realism and practicality as well as to increase learner participation, enjoyment, and retention. A case study allows the learner to practice or rehearse how to handle a new situation in a low-risk setting. Case studies are beneficial and successful when they

- allow learners to **discover new concepts,**
- are **non-threatening,** and
- build on past **experiences.**

Frequently, adult learners enjoy discovering new concepts by **arriving at their own conclusions,** rather than being told what to think or do and how to do a task. Learners are more likely to use and apply new concepts when they have studied and considered a situation and independently arrived at a conclusion. Often by discussing a case study, adult learners will change their minds and allow themselves to be influenced by peers. Ownership of an idea is more likely to occur when it is discovered, rather than heard from a trainer.

Case study situations can be a low-risk or **non-threatening** method for adults to learn from past experience, apply new knowledge or skills, and even rehearse or practice how to effectively change their behavior. With a case study, adults are not put in an awkward position of defending poor past practices. There is little risk in discussing a new idea or new method of doing a task.

Adult learners use their **experience** as a filter through which they learn new knowledge and skills and consider altering their attitudes. Mature or experienced learners who have been doing a specific task in a particular way (even incorrectly) prefer to learn through experience rather than being told directly that they are doing something wrong. A case study allows them to reach their own conclusions and to apply past learning.

Cautions

An effective case study must be realistic and authentic. The situation must be believable and parallel to the learner's situation. A case study needs to be authentic, but not so close to reality that the learner can identify specific co-workers or organizational folklore in negative situations. However, if a case is not at all authentic or realistic, participants may argue with the details of the case and miss the major learning points.

Examples of the Five Types of Case Studies

The next few pages show examples of the five types of case studies described above. For each case study the purpose is given, followed by directions to the learners and questions to consider, explore, and discuss following independent reading of the case.

At the end of each case are questions for the facilitator to ask as he or she leads a discussion of that particular case. These facilitator questions are designed to complete the learning process by helping the learners identify the concepts and apply what is learned.

Identification

CASE STUDY EXAMPLE

The purpose of this diagnostic case study is for the learner to identify what this new supervisor is doing that is appropriate or inappropriate. After identifying these behaviors, the learner (a new supervisor) can identify what similar behaviors he or she is doing or not doing and how to be more successful.

CASE STUDY 1: SUE WELDON, NEW SUPERVISOR

Directions: As you read the case Study,

- *Underline the things you think Sue is doing correctly.*
- *Bracket [ ] the things you think Sue is doing incorrectly.*
- *Decide if you would like Sue to work for you or if you would like to work for Sue.*

Sue Weldon is a highly regarded charge nurse and a bit of a perfectionist. She was promoted into a supervisory position six months ago because she is one of the best surgical staff nurses at the Medical Center.

Sue is a methodical planner and closely supervises the unit that helps patients recover from surgery. Sue says, "It's my job to get employees to provide the best patient care possible and do that in the most cost-effective manner possible. If anyone is doing something wrong, I tell him or her exactly what to do. I have learned to size up a problem quickly. I'm concerned about quality care for our patients. I have learned to get to the heart of the matter. My biggest problem is getting the rest of the staff to focus on care delivery. There's so much emphasis on cost containment. They must remember we're here to help patients recover from surgery and be well enough by the time they are discharged."

Upper management respects Sue for her good judgment. Sue tends to think through an issue and then make all of the decisions herself. Sue believes she is pretty good at selling her decisions to her staff. A major concern is losing authority over her staff, so she is loathe to admit making a mistake. When an employee does an excellent job, Sue is quick to compliment them. She is often concerned about solving problems, and when she finds the guilty party, her facts are listed in rapid fire order and her criticism can be sharp, often in front of others.

Employees complain Sue seldom asks their opinions on anything. They feel neglected and ignored.

The Unit rarely fails to meet its targets and always gets high marks on patient satisfaction surveys. To make sure productivity and satisfaction levels remain high, Sue frequently stays beyond the end of her shift to finish a job and complete planning tasks. Medical Center administration is pleased with Sue's Unit, but the Vice President of Nursing is concerned that Sue is working excessive overtime and it could affect her health.

Facilitator Processing Questions

What are the behaviors of an effective supervisor?

What circumstances make it easy or difficult for a new supervisor to be effective with subordinates?

How can a new supervisor overcome some of the barriers to supervising others?

What characteristics are important for you to develop?

How will you do that?

Problem Solving

CASE STUDY EXAMPLE

The purpose of this case study is to solve a problem by identifying the problem, creating a plan, and taking action. This case helps the learner sort out rumors from fact as part of the information-gathering step in problem solving.

CASE STUDY 2: RUMORS ABOUND!

Directions: Identify your plan of action to address the problem presented in the following case.

You have been hearing rumors that there are major complaints with the filing of correspondence in your department. Files everyone uses are missing, people waste hours of precious time trying to locate files, and the sign-out system is ignored by just about everyone. Because you work for the department manager, this issue has landed on your desk and your boss has told you to "fix it." When you begin to talk to others with access about the files, it is difficult to find anyone who has heard a complaint or is aware of the situation.

Facilitator Processing Questions

What is the problem?

What are the elements of the problem you want to uncover by your investigation?

What actions will you take to resolve the problem in looking for missing files?

Is your plan of action realistic?

What problems might occur if you implemented this plan?

What else could you do to solve this problem?

Are those involved in the problem likely to accept your plan of action?

What did you learn about planning to solve problems from this situation?

What are you likely to do when faced with similar problems?

Practice

CASE STUDY EXAMPLE

The skill being practiced is directing the work of others with the appropriate amount of direction. Giving orders can be done by offering information, making suggestions, making requests, or making commands. The case helps the learner read a problem all the way through to realize the possible consequences of some actions. The case also helps the learner recognize that effective direction is done with the **least** amount of control.

CASE STUDY 3: GIVING ORDERS

Directions: Read the following situation. Answer the five questions to prepare for a discussion with others.

Your manager has asked you to arrange the conference room for an orientation to your company of a group of very important visitors. There will be about twenty people attending the meeting and you want to make a good impression. Because several offices have been moved recently, the conference room has been used to store boxes. Making such arrangements is not part of your duties, but no one else is available at the moment.

You have asked two people to help you set up the room. One of them, Mary, is with you. She is your new support person. Jim, a custodian, has not shown up yet. The meeting will take place in two hours. In addition to some heavy cartons, the room is overcrowded with chairs and is dusty. You envision seating the visitors around the conference table. A slide presentation will be shown on the front wall; no screen is available.

1. You have an idea of how you want to arrange the room. Write down exactly what you would say to Mary in one sentence.
2. You decide to first clear the area for the projector. You want Mary to help you move some heavy cartons. What do you say to Mary?
3. After you have been dusting chairs for 20 minutes, Jim shows up. Working has been difficult because the room is overcrowded with cartons. What do you say to Jim?
4. Jim is trying to lift a heavy carton by himself, instead of asking for help or using a hand truck (which is downstairs). You are concerned Jim will hurt his back. What do you say?
5. Finally the room looks as it should. You sit down in one of the chairs to rest a bit, and notice that the wall directly opposite the projector has an electrical box in the center of it. It will be impossible to show the presentation on that wall. The table will have to be moved down and the projector moved to the other end of the room. What do you say to Jim and Mary?

Facilitator Processing Questions

What made it easy or difficult to find the right words to give orders to a new support person?

How is giving directions different when the person receiving your direction doesn't report to you?

What did you learn about giving directions from this exercise?

Application

CASE STUDY EXAMPLE

Prior to reading this case study, the learner has studied skills for managing a training function in a two-day workshop. The case helps the training manager apply a variety of skills through this summary activity including: identifying training needs, prioritizing projects, allocating resources, budgeting for training, and building alliances in the operation.

CASE STUDY 4: PRIORITIZE TRAINING PROJECTS

Directions: Review the set of circumstances and conditions described in the following case, then answer these questions:

- *What are your objectives for training?*
- *What is your recommendation to the Vice President of Operations (your boss)? Include recommendations for:*
  - *The type of training*
  - *Target population*
  - *Delivery system (centralized vs. road trip for general office trainer; self-paced video; outside seminars; train store managers as trainers; etc.)*
  - *The number of people you need to add to your staff of three (a course designer, an instructor, a support person).*

You are the training manager of "Catch Us Now," a small fast food chain that specializes in seafood. You have twenty-five outlets in major southern California cities, Nevada, and Arizona. The General Office is located in southern California. The company has committed to opening one new store per month for twenty-four months—the size will double in two years.

Cashier/counter server turnover is 60%. Currently, store managers barely have the time to interview cashiers, let alone train them. They are begging for help in recruitment and training of cashiers/servers. Of the 40% cashiers/counter servers who remain, some feel promotions go to those with connections in high places. They feel they are the "work horses" who hold the company together.

New store managers are promoted from within. The average age of store managers is 27. The Regional Manager does training for new store managers on an as-needed basis. Two years ago a manual was developed on how to run and manage a store. It needs updating.

Each store has about twenty cashier/counter servers and cooks. Brief job descriptions exist for each position, but procedure manuals are very brief. No effective orientation program exists.

About eight months ago the store managers completed a mandatory interviewing seminar. The chain is still experiencing several problems from "bad" hires. Grievances are still at too high a rate. Little improvement has come about in this area.

You are suspicious that the interviewing class may not have been as effective as you would have liked. The managers were enthusiastic, but the interviewing class was mostly lecture. It began with scare tactics about previous lawsuits and losses the company has suffered because of bad hires. The managers received handout materials that gave "chapter and verse" about legal questions to ask. This material was reviewed quickly and was basically included as "reference."

Answer the questions in the directions at the beginning of the case study.

Facilitator Processing Questions

What information led you to decide how to prioritize these training issues?

How do the proposed recommendations support the objectives you developed for this situation?

What additional information needs developing to allow you to finish the plan?

What did you learn about prioritizing training issues from this case?

How will you use these skills in the future?

Serial

CASE STUDY EXAMPLE

The purpose of this type of case study is to develop a series of skills by adding information to an on-going situation. In the first part of the case study, the Training Manager plans to build a partnership with the managers of the learners who will attend training. The Training Manager identifies what needs to be done before, during, and after the training to build the partnership. After additional skills are learned, the case situation is revisited two more times to apply skills being taught in the Training Manager workshop. Serial case studies have the advantage of building on previous information and added information helps bring sophistication and nuances to learning.

CASE STUDY 5, PART 1: MANAGER'S ROLE

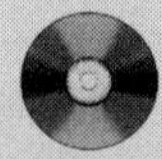

Directions: Read the information about the business need, training plan, and target population and identify appropriate tasks and roles for the Store Manager before, during, and after Product Knowledge *training.*

Situation: Fine Jewelry Retail Chain Requests Training for Retail Associates

The business need for a fine jewelry store chain is to increase retail sales, particularly on higher-priced products.

The training plan calls for interactive *Product Knowledge* training for Retail Associates. The training was designed at the corporate office in half-day modules to be conducted at the Regional Training Centers by Corporate Trainers assigned to each region. Role-play practice to sell higher-priced products is included in each module. A prerequisite for the *Product Knowledge* training is completion of *Selling Skills* training that is conducted monthly at the Regional Training Centers. Not all Retail Associates have attended *Selling Skills* training. Some Managers say their stores are short staffed and don't have the coverage to release new Associates to attend training outside the store.

The target population is two groups of Retail Associates: (1) sophisticated and experienced at selling fine jewelry (average age 38), or (2) young and inexperienced (average age 24). This younger group finds selling expensive jewelry difficult because they cannot afford such products for themselves.

If the chain is to meet the business need, identify the appropriate roles and tasks for the Store Managers before, during, and after *Product Knowledge* training.

Facilitator Processing Questions

What roles and tasks did you identify for the Store Managers before, during, and after *Product Knowledge* training?

What helped or hindered you in identifying these roles?

What additional information do you need to better identify these roles?

In general, what does a Store Manager need to do to support a training effort to get the desired results from training?

In your organization, what can be done to encourage managers to support a training effort to produce the desired results?

CASE STUDY 5, PART 2: MANAGERS SUPPORT THEIR OWN CHANGE

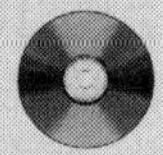

Directions: Using the "Fine Jewelry Product Knowledge Training for Retail Associates" case study, part 1, identify the changes in knowledge, attitude, and individual behavior that need to take place ***for the Store Managers*** *in order for their Associates' learning to transfer to the workplace.*

Knowledge changes:

Attitude changes:

Behavior changes:

Identify the following about the Store Managers:

1. Identify their probable level of commitment to these changes:
   - ___ Commitment (eager dedication, initiative, and willing participation)
   - ___ Genuine compliance (willingness and agreement with goals at the direction of others)
   - ___ Formal compliance (will complete as part of one's job)
   - ___ Grudging compliance (will complete only to keep a job)
   - ___ Non-compliance (not willing)
2. What amount of resistance is likely to occur that could be a barrier to transfer?
3. Which strategies will be critical to overcome that resistance?
4. What other strategies do you suggest that have not been discussed previously?

Facilitator Processing Questions

Given the changes in knowledge, attitude, and behavior that have just been discussed, what might it take to increase the Store Managers' commitment and reduce resistance to changes?

How realistic are the strategies to overcome resistance by Store Managers?

What are the characteristics of helpful strategies to overcome resistance to change by managers?

What can be done in your organization to overcome resistance to change by managers in your organization?

CASE STUDY 5, PART 3: MANAGERS SUPPORT ASSOCIATES' CHANGE

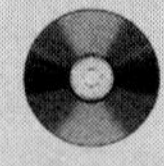

Directions: Using the "Fine Jewelry Product Knowledge Training for Retail Associates" case study, parts 1 and 2, identify the changes in knowledge, attitude, and individual behavior that need to take place ***for the Retail Associates*** *in order for their learning to transfer to the workplace.*

Knowledge changes:

Attitude changes:

Behavior changes:

Identify the following about the learners (Retail Associates):

1. Identify their probable level of commitment to these changes:

   ___ Commitment

   ___ Genuine compliance

   ___ Formal compliance

   ___ Grudging compliance

   ___ Non-compliance

2. What kind of resistance is likely to occur that could be a barrier to transfer?
3. Which manager strategies will be critical to overcome that resistance?
4. What other strategies do you suggest that have not been discussed previously?

Facilitator Processing Questions

Given the changes that the Retail Associates need to make and their level of commitment, how realistic are the strategies to overcome resistance to these changes?

What differences are there between strategies to overcome resistance of managers and their subordinates?

What have you learned about overcoming resistance and effective strategies through the three progressive case studies?

How can these strategies be applied in your organization?

SUMMARY

This chapter helped you:
Define case study, as a description of a situation the learner examines to increase knowledge and skills or influence attitudes.

Describe the Purpose of the Five Types of Case Studies:

1. Identification
2. Problem Solving
3. Practice
4. Application
5. Serial

Identify the Benefits of Using Case Studies:

- Add a note of realism and practicality as well as to increase learner participation, enjoyment, and retention.
- Allow the learner to practice or rehearse how to handle a new situation in a low-risk setting.

Identify Cautions When Developing Case Studies:

- Make case studies realistic when the situation is believable and parallels the learner's situation.
- Make case studies authentic, but not so close to reality that the learners can identify specific co-workers in negative situations. If the case is not authentic, participants may argue with the details of the case and miss the major learning points.

Finally, examples of the five types of case studies were presented. The next chapter will help develop an understanding of the process of writing or customizing a case study.

WHAT'S IN THIS CHAPTER?

After reading this chapter, you will be able to:

Use the eight-step process to write an original case study:

1. Write a learning objective.
2. Select one of the five types of case studies based on the objective.
3. Select the setting and characters needed to reach the objective.
4. Add dialogue if appropriate.
5. Write directions and discussion questions.
6. Test the case study and get feedback.
7. Revise the case study based on feedback.
8. Develop variations for different groups using the same case study.

Identify some problems in developing case studies and learn how to overcome them:

- Too much detail
- Too many points
- Too close to reality (people and/or situation)

Use templates, forms, and worksheets (on the CD) in this chapter including:

- Writing a case study
- Using a critique sheet to review a case study
- Customizing an existing case study

Use the suggested learner discussion questions for each type of case study (on the CD)

Use the suggested facilitator processing questions (on the CD)

2

How to Write a Case Study

Where Do Case Studies Fit in Workshop Design?

Prior to writing or customizing an existing case study for inclusion in a specific training program, basic elements of training program design need to be followed. There should be a business need established for conducting the training. The course designer needs to have completed a target population assessment to gather enough information about the needs of the group and their prior knowledge, skill level, and experience with the subject of the training program. Also, the course designer needs to perform a job/task analysis to identify the best way to complete the work. Once learning objectives are written and a course content outline is developed, the course designer can select a variety of interactive methods to meet the learning objectives. A means of measuring the outcomes of the training program is also developed as part of the course development planning process.

If you, as course developer, decide that using a case study is the most appropriate method of reaching the learning objective, use the eight-step method that follows to write an original case study or customize a case for inclusion in a specific training program.

How Do You Develop a Case Study?

There are eight steps in case study development.

1. Write a learning objective
2. Select one of the five types of case studies based on the objective
3. Select the setting and characters needed to reach the objective
4. Add dialogue if appropriate
5. Write directions and discussion questions
6. Test the case study and get feedback
7. Revise the case study based on feedback
8. Develop variations for different groups using the same case

Here is a description of the eight steps in case study development. A template to make case study development easier follows the description.

1. Write a learning objective.

You will be more effective in writing a case study if you identify a specific learning objective and keep the target population in mind when writing the objective. A clear objective will help you reach the desired outcome and focus the discussion appropriately. The following are effective objectives:

1. Write from the learner's point of view
2. Identify a specific behavior the learner performs
3. Describe the condition or circumstance for using the case
4. Describe the level of achievement (quality, quantity, or speed) you expect from the learners

Here is a sample learning objective for the diagnostic case study example in chapter 1 entitled, "Sue Weldon, New Supervisor." After discussing the case study in a small group [(3), condition], the supervisors [(1), written from learner's point of view] will be able to identify behaviors and characteristics of an effective supervisor [(2), specific behavior] and list three appropriate steps to increase personal effectiveness as a supervisor [(4), level of achievement, quality, and quantity].

When you use adjectives like "appropriate" to describe the level of achievement, have a model in mind. Define words like *appropriate;* and help the learners discover the model as part of their discussion. In this case study, an appropriate strategy to increase personal effectiveness would include a strategy to overcome one or more pitfalls of new supervisors.

2. Select one of the five types of case studies based on the objective. After writing a specific learning objective for the case study, identify which of the five types of case studies will best help the learners to discover the concept or learning point behind the case study. Several questions that will help you select the right type of case study follow.

Identification: What characteristics or points will be identified? Will both positive and negative characteristics be identified as part of the learning process? As part of the learning process, will the learner be asked to identify the characteristics or points from the case that they find in themselves?

Problem Solving: What is the problem the learner will solve? What problem-solving model will be used to solve the problem? What problem-solving skills does the target population already have that they can apply to this issue? Will elements of systematic and creative problem-solving techniques be used in the case? What steps in the problem-solving process do the learners complete? For example, will the problem be identified for the learner so the learner focuses on finding a solution, or is part of the case study to clearly identify the problem?

Practice: What skills will the learners practice? What new ideas will the learners discuss? Which attitudes are the case intended to influence? What is the sequence of multiple skills? Will the learners be able to identify assumptions made by the characters in the case? Will the learners be asked to identify prerequisites as a part of the practice?

Application: What are the elements to summarize and apply a set of complex ideas and/or skills that appear in this case? How are the elements of the case related to each other? Is the sequence of elements an issue in this case? Will learners prioritize the elements of the case to demonstrate what has been learned? What is the setting in which the learners will apply a set of complex ideas or skills?

Serial: Which elements from the preceding four types of cases can be combined to develop a progression of skills? What is the progression of elements that will be developed? Will the case study developer need to use a task analysis and skill hierarchy to help sequence the progression of ideas, concepts, and skills?

3. Select the setting and characters needed to reach the objective. After writing an objective and selecting the appropriate type of case study, select the setting and characters that are likely to reach the learning objective. Consider a setting that closely parallels the learner's situation. Factors include:

- Where learners work: Industry, government, or non-profit organization
- Reporting relationships: type of work groups or team environment
- Collective bargaining organization or lack of it
- Size and scope of the setting
- Physical setting

Industry-specific settings help the learner easily identify with the situation. For example, employees in a manufacturing setting prefer to read case studies set in a manufacturing plant that resembles their workplace. Successful settings also resemble reporting relationships. For example, employees who work in a team environment usually have a team leader rather than a supervisor, which is usually the case in a work group with a more rigid hierarchy. Those who work in a union shop prefer case studies that mirror their environment. The size and scope of the setting refer to whether a case is set in an organization, a division, a department, a work group, or between two individuals. If the physical setting makes a difference, it would describe the location of the interaction that is the focus of the case study. For example, a bank employee could meet the customer in a teller line, at the drive-up teller window, or on the telephone. The interaction between two individuals might take place in an office, on the shop floor, at the customer's place of business, or in the break room. When choosing the setting, it needs to parallel the learner's situation so the learners can focus on the learning point and not be distracted with an unfamiliar setting.

When selecting characters for a case study, consider whether these elements make sense in reaching the learning objective of a particular case:

- Job titles of characters
- Age, sex, and cultural background of characters
- Whether to give names to characters
- Knowledge, skills, and attitudes of characters

Effective job titles parallel the learner's experience. If salesclerks are called associates in the learner's workplace, call them associates in the case study. If most of the target population reading a case study are Hispanic females in their 50s, then make the characters familiar to the audience by creating a character with those attributes. Learners ought to be able to identify with the characters in the case as typical of their situation.

Create characters that are believable without specific individuals being recognizable. Names ought to reflect the typical character in the organization. If a character does not have a name, refer to the character by job title. Be careful not to use stereotypes or show ethnic bias in selecting and naming characters.

4. Add dialogue if appropriate.

Writing dialogue that sounds natural is difficult. If your dialogue is believable and typical of the character and contributes to the purpose of the case, then use it. If you think the dialogue does not sound natural or authentic or might distract learners, leave it out. Effective case studies usually come from developing the setting and the characters, rather than the words the character says.

5. Write directions and discussion questions.

Write directions for the reader to prepare for a discussion. Written directions at the beginning of the case study tell the learner what to look for or what to prioritize or in some way judge the information that follows. For example, the identification case study in chapter 1 asked the reader to "Underline the things you think Sue is doing correctly; bracket the things you think Sue is doing incorrectly; decide if you would like Sue to work for you or if you would like to work for Sue." Repeat the same questions at the end of the case study if you expect the learner to answer them in writing prior to a discussion.

After the learners discuss the case study questions, ask additional questions to develop and apply the concept behind the case study. Write questions for the facilitator to ask. These questions are entitled, "Facilitator Processing Questions" throughout this book. See the five sample case studies in chapter 1 for some processing questions and also see the template and list of questions at the end of this chapter for the five different types of case studies.

6. Test the case study and get feedback.

Write a test scenario for the case study. Is it realistic without being too close to home? Will the learners achieve the learning objective or purpose of the case through the setting and characters in the case? Are questions appropriately worded to encourage discussion of relevant issues? Is the dialogue between characters helpful rather than distracting? Have both peers (others who know something about case study construction) and target population give feedback on the case. A template of a critique sheet to assess the effectiveness of a case study is provided later in this chapter.

7. Revise the case study based on feedback.

Based on the feedback from peers and the target population, identify changes that are appropriate for the case study. You do not need to implement every suggestion. Sometimes suggested revisions are a matter of style, rather than substance. Identify those revisions that make sense and will actually improve the case study.

8. Develop variations for different groups using the same case study.

Finally, consider creating different versions of the same case study so you can use an existing case study in another course with a few changes. For example, several departments may be attending the same workshop and by changing the setting to another department, you can use the case study effectively for a different target population. See the template on customizing a case study later in this chapter.

How to Overcome Problems in Developing Case Studies

When developing or customizing a case study, pay attention to these types of problems:

- Too much detail
- Too many points cause confusion
- Too close to reality (people and/or situation)

Learners frequently need fewer details than the real situation to meet the learning objective. If the objective of the case study can be accomplished in one paragraph instead of three and still make the same point, use one paragraph. Too many details about a situation can cause confusion and divert attention from the points that need discussion so the learners reach the objective of the case study.

The purpose of the first three types of case studies (identification, problem solving, and practice) is to help the learners discuss one aspect of an issue. Narrow the setting and the characters to focus on the specific point the learners are to discover. When case studies focus on several points, learners can become confused and may spend discussion time sorting out several pieces of information that will not help them reach the learning objective. It is often easier to write two or three serial case studies than combine all the points into one complex case study.

Keep in mind that a case study needs to be natural, familiar, and authentic while **not** duplicating the real situation. To create characters that are believable without being able to recognize the identity of specific individuals, combine several attributes into the same character or change the age, sex, or physical attributes of the character. The combination of attributes makes the character easier to discuss and the learners will recognize the purpose of the case more easily. When learners recognize characters or a specific situation, the learning point is often forgotten and case study discussions can become gossip sessions.

Templates

Three templates are provided to help the case study developer use the suggestions in this chapter. The templates include:

- Case Study Checklist (eight steps to write a case study).
- Case Study Critique Sheet that uses a point system to identify weak areas needing redesign
- Customize a Case Study Worksheet to redesign an existing case study

CASE STUDY CHECKLIST

Use this eight-step process to write a case study.

1. Write a learning objective.

   "Given a case study, the ______ [insert learner's job title] will be able to ______ [insert specific behavior], and ______ [insert the level of achievement: quality, quantity, or speed]."

2. Select one of the five types of case studies based on the objective.

   - Identification
   - Problem solving
   - Practice
   - Application
   - Serial

3. Select the setting and characters needed to reach the objective.

   Setting:

   - Where learners work: industry, government, or non-profit organization
   - Reporting relationships: type of work groups or team environment
   - Collective bargaining organization or lack of it
   - Size and scope of the setting
   - Physical setting

   Characters:

   - Job titles of characters
   - Age, sex, and cultural differences of characters
   - Whether to give names to characters
   - Knowledge, skills, and attitudes of characters

4. Add dialogue if appropriate.

5. Write directions and discussion questions including:
    - Clear directions to set up the case study
    - Specific questions to answer as the case is discussed
    - Appropriate facilitator questions to process learning points
6. Test the case study and get feedback.
7. Revise the case study based on feedback.
8. Develop variations for different groups using the same case study.

CASE STUDY CRITIQUE SHEET

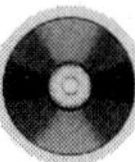

Directions: Read the case study and rate the completeness of each element based on the following scale:

0 = element is absent

1 = minimal element or confused information

2 = sufficient information

3 = appropriate information

_____ Learning objective has all four elements (written from learner's point of view, specific behavior, condition, and level of achievement).

_____ Appropriate type of case study selected. If not appropriate, suggest a different type of case study: ______________________________ (identification, problem solving, practice, application, serial)

_____ Setting specific enough to reach the objective (Industry, reporting relationships, union/non-union, size/scope, physical setting)

_____ Characters specific enough to reach the objective (Job titles, age, sex, cultural differences, names of characters, knowledge, skills, attitudes represented)

_____ Dialogue appropriate

_____ Directions are clear

_____ Questions for learners are appropriate

_____ Facilitator questions are appropriate and develop learning points

_____ Total points (total scores under 14 need revision to achieve the objective)

Suggested revisions to this case:

CUSTOMIZE A CASE STUDY WORKSHEET

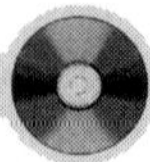

Case studies can be more effective when used with a new target audience by customizing the setting, characters, dialogue, directions, and questions. Use this form to consider points to customize an existing case study. Answer these questions about the new target audience:

_____ Is the **learning objective** the same as provided in the existing case? If not, is this the appropriate case study for the learning point that participants will discover?

_____ Is the **type** of case study appropriate for the new target audience? Is a different type of case study more appropriate?

_____ What parts of the setting need to be customized? Is the setting too close to reality?

- Where learners work
- Reporting relationships
- Collective bargaining setting or not
- Size and scope of the case
- Physical setting

_____ What elements of the case study's characters need to be customized? Are they too close to reality?

- Job titles of characters
- Age, sex, cultural differences
- Character's names
- Knowledge, skills, and attitudes of characters

_____ What parts of the dialogue need to be customized?

_____ What parts of the directions need to be customized?

_____ What discussion questions need to be customized or added?

_____ What facilitator questions need to be customized or added?

Sample Questions for the Five Types of Case Studies

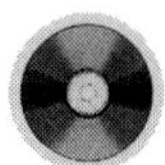

When writing a case study, choose appropriate questions for the learner to answer that will lead to the point the learner is to discover through the case study. Consider selecting the following types of discussion questions for each type of case study and make the questions part of the directions to the learner.

Identification

- What is the person in the case doing correctly/incorrectly?
- What problems result from how the person in the case handles each issue?
- What other approaches do you recommend to be more effective?

Problem Solving

- What is the main problem?
- What are the symptoms of the problem versus the causes of the problem?
- Are there issues that may not be problems and do not require your attention?
- What are the possible solutions in this case?
- What are the advantages/disadvantages of each solution?
- What is your plan of action?
- What do you recommend?

Practice

- What is the skill you are using?
- How easy/difficult is it to use this skill?

- What makes it easy or difficult to use this skill?
- What helps or hinders using these ideas or skills?
- What are the problems you encounter when trying out this skill?
- How can you overcome the difficulties in using this skill?
- What are the building blocks to using this skill?
- If you are willing to re-evaluate your attitude toward this skill, what is another perspective you have gained in using this skill?

Application

- What are the key points in making this issue successful?
- How are the key points interrelated?
- What are the critical elements of success?
- What are the barriers to being successful?
- How can you overcome these barriers?
- How can you prioritize the lesson learned from this case for your situation?
- What are the consequences of not paying attention to primary issues in this case?
- What skills help you overcome the barriers in this case?
- How will you realistically apply this skill in your setting?

Serial

- How do successive knowledge, skills, and attitudes build upon each other?
- What insights have you gained from successive knowledge or skills in this case?
- Given hindsight, what could you have done sooner to be more successful in solving the issues of this case?

Facilitator Processing Questions to Promote Learning

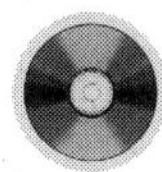

After learners have discussed the questions about the learning points in the case study, the facilitator needs to ask additional questions to meet the learning objective. Learners need to reflect on the case study and share their reactions with each other as a transition step to move from the case situation to recognizing what they have learned. Once general concepts have been learned, participants can then apply what is learned to their own situations. Facilitator processing questions are not shown to the learner as part of the case study; rather they are given to the facilitator as part of a lesson plan with suggested answers.

Here are several questions to facilitate discussing learning points:

Facilitator Processing Questions for Learners to Share and Interpret Their Reactions to the Activity

- What happened when you tried out that function/step as part of the case?
- What surprised you?
- What part was easy? Difficult? What made it easy? Difficult?
- What did you notice/observe? How was that significant?
- How was that positive/negative?
- What struck you most about that?
- How do these pieces fit together?

Facilitator Processing Questions for Learners to Identify Concepts from Their Reactions

- How does this relate to other parts of the process?
- What might we conclude from that?
- What did you learn/relearn?

- What processes/steps are similar to this one?
- What else is this step/process like?
- What does that suggest to you about __________ in general?
- What's important to remember about this step/function?
- What other options/ways do you have for completing this step/function?
- How can you integrate this step into the larger process?
- What other functions are impacted by this step?

Facilitator Processing Questions for Learners to Apply Concepts to Their Situation

- How can you use this?
- What is the value of this step/function?
- What would be the consequence of doing/not doing this?
- What changes can you make to help it work for you?
- How does that fit with your experience?

SUMMARY

Identify the Eight-Step Process to Write an Original Case Study:

1. Write a learning objective.
2. Select one of the five types of case studies based on the objective.
3. Select the setting and characters needed to reach the objective.
4. Add dialogue if appropriate.
5. Write directions, discussion questions, and facilitation questions.
6. Test the case study and get feedback.
7. Revise the case study based on feedback.
8. Develop variations for different groups using the same case study.

Problems in Developing Case Studies and How to Overcome Them:

- Too much detail
- Too many points
- Too close to reality (people and/or situation)

Templates, Forms, and Worksheets in This Chapter:

- Case study checklist
- Critique sheet to review a case study
- Customize an existing case study

Appropriate Discussion Questions

Facilitator Processing Questions

WHAT'S IN THIS CHAPTER?

After reading this chapter, you will be able to:

Facilitate a case study discussion using a five-step adult learning process that includes how the:

1. Facilitator sets up the case study
2. Participants discuss the case study
3. Participants share their reactions to and interpretations of the case study
4. Participants identify the concepts from the case study
5. Participants apply learning concepts from the case study to their jobs

Write questions to process a case study so learners discover the point of the case study

Use the following ten facilitation techniques appropriately while processing a case study:

1. Initiate a case study discussion.
2. Divide learners into subgroups to discuss a case study.
3. Use questioning to draw learners out, and elicit information and opinions about the case study.
4. Use silence to make space.
5. As learners report on their discussion, keep track of multiple topics and build on the ideas of others.
6. Use flip charting to generate additional discussion of case study learning points and record ideas.
7. Listen for common themes developed in a case study discussion and bar irrelevant details and redirect discussion to focus on case study concepts.
8. Organize the sequence of speakers.
9. Paraphrase to clarify or show understanding.
10. Have learners relate specific examples to a general idea or make a summary.

3

How to Facilitate a Case Study

Using Your Case Studies in Training

Five Steps of Adult Learning

Now that you have written a case study that illustrates your learning point, you will use it within the context of a successful training event.

This is a general description of what takes place during the five steps of adult learning. The successful facilitator guides adult learners through these five steps to gain the most from a case study and achieve the learning objective. These five steps are similar to many experiential learning models.

1. Set up the learning activity within which you will use the case.

For a case study to be successful, set up the case study so the participants understand **what** they are going to do (read a case study and individually prepare answers for a discussion) and **why** they are doing it. Adult learners become motivated when they understand the benefit to them of learning something new or the importance of a case study discussion for themselves. To this end, give directions and ground rules regarding how the case study discussion is to be conducted. The set-up of using a case study as a learning activity can include such things as:

- Tell participants the purpose of the case study discussion and why they are going to learn from the case study without giving away what is to be "discovered"
- Explain what the participants are going to do
- Review the written directions and questions to prepare the case study individually
- Divide participants into small groups
- Assign small group roles such as recorder, reporter, small group discussion leader
- Give other ground rules

2. Have learners read the case and prepare answers to the questions and discuss the questions in small groups.

For a case study discussion to be successful, involve learners as much as possible. Consider how learning from a case study will appeal to different learning styles. This step includes individual reading of a case study, following the written directions given at the beginning of the case study, preparing answers to discussion questions, and discussing the questions. Following the learners' discussion, ask a reporter from each small group to share each group's answers.

3. Have learners share and interpret their reactions to the case.

This step is essential to help conclude the small group case study discussions and gives learners the opportunity to identify what happened in different small group discussions. Ask the group additional questions to help the learners analyze the discussion, and then develop individual and group reactions to the activity. Learners share their reactions by identifying what happened to themselves and others, and how his/her behavior affected others during the small group discussion. Sample facilitator processing questions are

- "What made it easy or difficult to find a solution to this problem?"
- "What helped or hindered the progress of the discussion?"
- "Let's summarize the key points from the case study."

Sometimes, it is appropriate to have participants individually write down their reaction to the case study discussion so that another person does not influence their thinking before sharing reactions to a case study. Reactions come from the learners, not the facilitator, so the learners can discover the concept behind the case study.

Sharing a reaction is the beginning step of developing a pattern. If some participants do not share their reactions, it is difficult to end the activity and "get out of the case." Learners may prolong some unfinished business that spills over into other activities during a workshop.

4. Have learners identify concepts from their reactions.

In this step, have learners move away from the specific situation or story in the case study. This is the "So what did I learn from the case study?" step. Questions that help learners develop concepts include:

- "What did you learn about how to conduct an interview (discipline a subordinate, teach a new job, etc.) from this case study?"
- "What is appropriate behavior for a new supervisor?"

If this step is left out, then learning will be incomplete and the objective might not be reached. Up to this point, participants have been actively learning from a specific situation, and may not be able to apply new learning to similar situations outside the classroom. When concepts are inferred from a case study discussion, adult learners are ready to apply these newly learned or recently confirmed concepts to future situations. For discovery learning to take place, ask questions to elicit concepts from the learners, rather than tell them the concepts they should have found in the case study.

5. Help learners apply concepts to their situation.

This is the "So what now?" step in the adult learning process. Ask participants how they can use and apply the new information they have learned from the case study discussion. Ask:

- "How will you use the skill in the case study the next time a subordinate asks you for a favor?"
- "What are some situations in which you would be more effective if you used this technique?"

If this step is left out, the learner may not see the relationship between the case study and his/her job or situation and consider what others learned as not useful to him/her. This step stresses practical application and helps the learner get a personal benefit from the case study.

To effectively facilitate a case study discussion, ask the learners questions about their case study discussion, rather than tell them suggested applications. In addition to answering specific questions about the case, questions for steps 3, 4, and 5 of the adult learning process are appropriate to encourage discovery learning. In the case study examples in chapter 1, these questions are called "Facilitator Processing Questions." Some additional sample questions for learning steps 3, 4, and 5 follow.

Facilitator Processing Questions

QUESTIONS FOR STEP 3: LEARNERS SHARE AND INTERPRET THEIR REACTIONS TO THE ACTIVITY

- What happened when you tried out that function/step as part of the case?
- What surprised you?
- What part was easy? Difficult? What made it easy? Difficult?
- What did you notice/observe? How was that significant?
- How was that positive/negative?
- What struck you most about that?
- How do these pieces fit together?

QUESTIONS FOR STEP 4: LEARNERS IDENTIFY CONCEPTS FROM THEIR REACTIONS

- How does this relate to other parts of the process?
- What might we conclude from that?
- What did you learn/relearn?
- What processes/steps are similar to this one?

- What else is this step/process like?
- What does that suggest to you about __________ in general?
- What's important to remember about this step/function?
- What other options/ways do you have for completing this step/function?
- How can you integrate this step into the larger process?
- What other functions are impacted by this step?

QUESTIONS FOR STEP 5: LEARNERS APPLY CONCEPTS TO THEIR SITUATION

- How can you use this?
- What is the value of this step/function?
- What would be the consequence of doing/not doing this?
- What changes can you make to help it work for you?
- How does that fit with your experience?

Using Basic Facilitation Techniques

Some basic facilitation skills are needed to process a case study discussion. Each of the following ten facilitation techniques are described along with what the technique might look or sound like when processing a case study. Ten facilitation techniques for leading a case study discussion are

1. Initiate a case study discussion.

Set the stage for the work the group needs to do by clarifying the case study discussion's original purpose and suggesting approaches to accomplish it. Use this technique:

- To start the discussion
- If the group needs to refocus
- If the group is running dry of ideas
- When the group is better at reacting than initiating

What might this technique look/sound like?

Say:

- *"I'd like to suggest we begin examining this case study by . . ."*
- *"Let's divide into small groups and brainstorm solutions for this case."*
- *"To get us started, let's review the directions at the top of the page and three questions at the end of the case."*
- *"I think there are still some ideas we haven't considered about this case study."*

2. Divide learners into subgroups to discuss a case study.

Increase involvement and energy by lowering the risk of participation and increasing the amount of "air time." Surface multiple aspects of a case study. Consider whether this technique will help meet the learning objective and how much time is allotted for this activity. Use this technique:

- When you want more participation
- To encourage quiet participants
- To provide a change of pace
- To explore an idea in greater depth
- When the risk of participating in large groups is too great
- To allow introverted participants an opportunity to think and speak in a smaller group

What might this technique look/sound like?

- Subgroup by numbering off, using playing cards, candy, table groups.
- Decide if you will give directions for the case study before learners move to groups or after.
- Assign recorder, reporter, and group leader roles or ask participants to identify these roles for themselves.

- Say, *"Let's spend a bit more time developing the ideas in this case study and divide into small groups to continue our discussion."*
- *Tell the group how much time they have to complete the directions at the beginning of the case study.*

3. Use questioning to draw learners out, and elicit information and opinions about the case study.

Create a comfortable opening for participants to share ideas, thoughts, and concerns about the case study. Use this technique:

- In the early stages of a discussion while participants are getting comfortable with the case study situation and each other
- To help the group stay divergent rather than focusing on one solution for a problem solving case study
- To get additional information
- To get additional opinions
- When ideas start to dry up or slow down

What might this technique look/sound like?

Ask:

- *"What are the concerns for applying this idea?"*
- *"How would you use the information in this case study?"*
- *"What has been your experience in similar situations raised in this case?"*
- *"How has the solution to this case study worked for you in the past?"*
- *"What are issues or problems that have surfaced in this case study?"*
- *"How does this case study compare to your situation?"*

4. Use silence to make space.

Pause to give participants the time to collect their thoughts and decide what they want to say and how they want to express it. Some case studies have complex ideas and need individual consideration before speaking.

Quiet participants may not be contributing for a variety of reasons. More verbal participants may intimidate them, they may be unsure of how their ideas will be received, or they may feel inferior to the group and not want to seem foolish or "not as smart" as others. Use this technique:

- To allow the participant to decide what point he/she wants to make about the case study
- When quiet participants need to think about answering a specific case study question
- When participants need to determine the personal risk of participating
- When you think the group knows the answer to a case study question
- To allow participants to get in touch with ideas and feelings elicited in the case study
- When a participant gives a factually incorrect answer not supported by information in the case study
- When participants are confused or agitated

What might this technique look/sound like?

- Stop talking.
- Don't ask another question.
- Don't rephrase the question already asked.
- Keep looking around the room for volunteers.
- Step backward from the group.
- Be near the flip chart, pen poised for the next answer.
- Stay relaxed and pay attention to body language.
- If you have to talk, say, *"Let's take a minute and silently think about what that means to you."*
- Hold up your hand to stop others from talking (if that's your intent).

- When you've asked a difficult open-ended question, you might say, *"I'll give you a few minutes of quiet to think about your answer."*

5. As learners report on their discussion, keep track of multiple topics and build on the ideas of others.

Keep track of the various elements of a case study being discussed and treat each as valid and worthy of discussion. Help the group round out its discussion by surfacing different points of view that may be present but have not been expressed. When you publicly keep track of the various issues it helps the participants stay involved and engaged. Use this technique:

- To help the group add ideas from their own experience to the group discussion
- To help the group stay divergent and avoid convergent thinking too soon, especially when discussing problem-solving case studies
- When the group gets stuck
- When the idea is incomplete and the case study is more complex than the group has discussed
- When others have expertise to add to the idea just expressed

What might this technique look/sound like?

- The facilitator or participants write ideas on a flip chart.
- Drawing arrows on the flip chart to show relationship to another's idea.
- Ask, *"How can you expand on that idea?"*
- Ask, *"What is the relationship between these two ideas?"*
- Ask, *"Who has had a similar experience as the one raised in this case study?"*
- Ask, *"What do the rest of you think about how the problem was solved in the case study?"*

6. Use flip charting to generate additional discussion of case study learning points and record ideas.

Charting learners' contributions to validate ideas, provide a record of a discussion, and stimulate new and often more creative ideas. Use this technique:

- To keep a visual reminder of concepts the learners draw out of the case study
- To acknowledge and demonstrate value in contributed ideas
- To help sort and organize ideas as they are collected
- To record concepts during the fourth step of the adult learning process
- To encourage participation and discussion
- To focus the discussion of the case study's main points

What might this technique look/sound like?

- Ask, *"Did I accurately record your idea?"*
- Write the participants' words or gain permission to alter them.
- Connect or group like kinds of ideas.
- Use more than one ink color to chart ideas or thoughts about the case study.
- Use symbols or icons to add emphasis and sort ideas.

7. Listen for common themes developed in a case study discussion and bar irrelevant details and redirect discussion to focus on case study concepts.

When different opinions or disagreements polarize a group it is difficult for learners to recognize they have anything in common. Set aside comments that are not relevant to this case study discussion, validate areas of disagreement, and focus on areas of agreement. Use this technique:

- When a contribution is unclear
- When a contribution is taking the group off track or is not related to the case study situation

- When time is critical
- When the participant is confused

What might this technique look/sound like?

- NOT writing a contribution on the flip chart or use the "parking lot" if you can use the idea elsewhere. The parking lot is a piece of blank easel paper used to "park" ideas for discussion at a more appropriate time.
- Ask the participant to relate his/her idea to the case study discussion.
- Say, *"Let's come back to our main point/objective of this case study."*
- Paraphrase the comment before barring it.
- Say, *"I'm not sure how this example relates to the objective of this case study."*

8. Organize the sequence of speakers.

When several participants indicate a desire to talk at the same time, publicly create a speaking order. This procedure relieves you of the responsibility of keeping track of who is to speak next. Use this technique:

- When several participants want to speak at once
- When participants are interrupting one another, vying for attention
- When the facilitator can't keep track personally of who has spoken and who is waiting to speak

What might this technique look/sound like?

- Start by asking all who want to speak on a particular topic to raise their hands.
- Create a speaking order: *"Linda, you're first. Gary, you're second and Kevin, you're third."*
- When Linda has finished, *"So, who was second? OK, Gary, your turn."*
- After Kevin, ask *"Who else would like to say something?"*

9. Paraphrase to clarify or show understanding.
Reveal what you think a participant meant or to clarify and validate an understanding. Ask for confirmation that you got it right. Use this technique:

- When participant information is unclear
- When the participant is upset and needs acknowledgement
- When a participant has been lengthy

What might this technique look/sound like?

- Convey your interest in understanding what another means by asking questions and/or ask for more information.
- Reveal what the other's statements mean to you by giving an example or rephrasing what the learner has said and how it related to this case study.

10. Have learners relate specific examples to a general idea or make a summary.
Support learners as they identify what is important in the case study, that is, what is really meant by the case study as it relates to the discussion's original purpose. Use this technique:

- When the group has had enough input and needs to develop a theme or main concept to be discovered in the case study
- When several ideas are "on the table" and no organization is apparent
- To eliminate confusion
- To make the example of greater value to others in the group without similar experience
- At the end of a case study, before a transition to the next content piece in a workshop
- Before a break or at the end of the day

- To be sure the group has the idea, especially if it is a foundation for future information
- When moving to the fourth or fifth step in the adult learning process

What might this technique look/sound like?

- Ask, *"We've heard several examples, is there a theme to them that is emerging from the case study?"*
- Ask, *"What is the larger idea behind that example/suggestion?"*
- Ask, *"Have other examples occurred that are similar to the one in this case study?"*
- Pointing to flip chart or overview graphic.
- Ask participants to identify major learning point of importance to them from the case study.
- Say, *"Let's review . . ."*
- Ask, *"What do you want to remember from this case study?"*
- Say, *"Before we leave for our break . . ."*
- Say, *"Let's go back and review what we've learned and compare that to the directions at the beginning of the case study."*

SUMMARY

The following are the key points in this chapter:

Using Case Studies in Training, Facilitate a Case Study Discussion Using a Five-Step Adult Learning Process That Includes:

1. Facilitator sets up the learning activity
2. Participants discuss the case study
3. Participants share their reactions to and interpretations of the case study
4. Participants identify the concepts from the case study
5. Participants apply learning concepts from the case study to their jobs

Write Questions to Process a Case Study

Using ten basic facilitation techniques to process a case study:

1. Initiate, propose, and make suggestions.
2. Divide learners into subgroups to discuss a case study.
3. Use questioning to draw people out, and elicit information and opinions about case studies.
4. Use silence to make space.
5. As learners report on their discussion, keep track of multiple topics and build on the ideas of others.
6. Use flip charting to generate additional discussion of case study learning points and record ideas.
7. Listen for common themes developed in a case study discussion and bar irrelevant details and redirect discussion to focus on case study concepts.
8. Organize the sequence of speakers.
9. Paraphrase to clarify or show understanding.
10. Have learners relate specific examples to a general idea or make a summary.

PART 2

Introduction to Part 2: Case Study Exercises

ALL of the case studies in part 2 of this book can be downloaded from the enclosed CD-ROM (CD) and customized to meet the objectives and needs of a specific training session. Directions and a template for customizing case studies are in part 1, chapter 2, page 42 and on the CD.

The chapters in part 2 are organized alphabetically by the training topic, that is, Adult Learning, Assertion, Change Management, and so on. Within each chapter are examples of the five types of case studies, as described earlier: Identification, Problem Solving, Practice, Application, Serial.

Each case study contains directions for the learner and questions for him or her to think about while reading the case study. Following each case study are

- The learning objective for the case study
- Possible answers to the questions posed in each case study
- Suggested facilitator processing questions
- Possible answers to the facilitator processing questions

The learning objective, case study answers, facilitator processing questions and answers are not on the CD. The learning objective is not on the CD for two reasons: First, the purpose of a case study is to allow the learner to discover ideas and apply skills. If the learner knows the objective of the case study, there is little left to discover. Second, the trainer can decide how well the case study objective matches the specific use for an individual case study. The objective can be changed to meet individual learning needs.

It's recommended that you **not** share facilitator processing questions in writing with the learners prior to their reading the case studies. Ask these questions after learners have read the case study and have answered the case questions or followed other directions to prepare for a case study discussion. That way, the learners are more likely to focus on the point of the case study prior to the discussion.

To prepare to facilitate a case study:

- Read the case study and review the learning objective to decide whether or not it is appropriate for your training situation, and whether or not it will meet the learners' needs.
- Decide whether to use the case study as it is written or which parts of the case study will be customized as suggested on page 42.
- Prepare the answers to the case study questions that accompany each case study. While some possible answers to case study questions are provided, the specific answers you are seeking may be different depending on how you wish to customize the case and on the group using the case study.
- Review the suggested "Facilitator Processing Questions and Potential Answers" and select those that will help make the learning points you wish to make for a specific class. These processing questions are intended to help the learners discover the concepts and apply them to their own situations. While potential answers are provided, additional interpretations and answers could emerge from your learners, your personal expertise, and/or from research.

4

Adult Learning Case Studies

THIS CHAPTER contains five types of case studies: Identification, Problem solving, Practice, Application, and Serial that teach various lessons about how adults learn and what helps adults learn and remember. Case studies in this chapter might be used in "train-the-trainer" workshops or to help those new to training to be more effective in handling new training responsibilities.

See the Introduction to Part 2 on pages 63–64 for suggestions on how to select and customize the case studies in this chapter.

ADULT LEARNING IDENTIFICATION CASE STUDY 6

What's Gone Wrong?

Directions: Read the following situation, and identify what's wrong with this training session.

The purchasing department manager began his training session by announcing his objective: "I will explain how the purchasing system works, how to navigate the software, and how I usually troubleshoot problems when buying large dollar items." He then darkened the room and proceeded to show a series of slides that paralleled his lecture. He frequently read to the group directly from the slides.

Participants were given handout materials that showed three slides per page to make their own notes. Participants were asked to hold their questions until the end of the session. He added, "Most of your questions will be answered during the training. So please be patient." The manager showed about forty slides during the first hour of the lecture. Two participants discussed their confusion about the topic in a noisy side conversation.

What's wrong here?

Facilitator Notes for Case Study 6

LEARNING OBJECTIVE: Given an identification case study and using their own experience, the learners will identify at least three adult learning concepts have been violated and plan how to honor adult learning principles in their own training sessions.

Possible Case Answers

What went wrong here?

- Darkened room and too many slides encourages inattention.
- Reading to the group from the slides is condescending.
- Participants were not allowed to ask clarifying questions when they occurred so side conversations developed.
- Troubleshooting is a skill and not easily addressed by offering information through lecture.

Facilitator Processing Questions and Possible Answers

Q: What adult learning concepts did the purchasing department manager violate?

A: Adult learning concepts violated include:

- Lack of participation by learners
- Darkened room encourages inattention
- Reading to the group from slides the learners can read for themselves
- Not allowing clarifying questions when they occur
- Permitting a noisy side conversation that distracted other learners

Q: What made it easy to identify these concepts?

A: These concepts are easy to identify because most of us have been forced to attend similar briefings that vaguely resemble a training session.

Q: Think of other situations when trainers you have observed violated adult learning principles. What caused these trainers to teach in this manner?

A: Learners will volunteer other examples from their experience. Trainers teach in this manner because most are imitating what they have seen others do and haven't been trained in the use of appropriate adult learning techniques.

Q: What are some adult learning concepts you want to be sure to incorporate into your training sessions?

A: These answers will vary depending on the needs of individual participants and which concepts are applicable for them.

ADULT LEARNING PROBLEM SOLVING CASE STUDY 7

Asking for Trouble

Directions: Read the case study, and from the description identify the problem. What are some of the adult learning issues and problems? What questions would you ask to try to identify the problem?

During the morning session of a workshop, new employees learn about the organization's policies and procedures for taking orders over the telephone. All but two employees seem to understand your directions and major points in the lecture. When you've asked them direct questions, they appear nervous and say they prefer to just listen and maybe participate in the discussion later.

The afternoon portion of the program is a lab session to introduce the order entry software that employees will use on a daily basis. Several employees are asking questions that will be answered later if they would be more patient. Later in the lab session, while conducting a demonstration no one asked any questions. Now that it's practice time to complete some lab exercises, you're disappointed that few employees can complete the lab correctly. Why didn't they just ask for help?

- What are some adult learning issues and/or problems?
- What are questions to ask of the instructor and the learners to help you identify the problem?

Facilitator Notes for Case Study 7

LEARNING OBJECTIVE: Given a case study, the learner will be able to identify at least three adult learning problems and possible remedies for the problems.

Possible Case Answers

What are some adult learning issues and/or problems?

- Learners are reluctant to participate and discuss questions.
- Learners are reluctant to ask questions, or when they asked questions were told to be more patient.
- Lecture and discussion seem like inappropriate methods to prepare for a skills lab.
- Few employees could complete the lab exercises correctly.

What are questions to ask of the instructor and the learners to help you identify the problem?

- What would help the learners be more successful?
- What other methods can be used more successfully to prepare learners for the skills lab?
- What causes learners to stop asking questions? How do you remedy that?
- What other methods can the instructor use to check for the learners' understanding?
- What can be done to involve learners in a demonstration?

Facilitator Processing Questions and Potential Answers

Q: How are problem participant behaviors related to the violation of adult learning principles?

A: Learners are not asking for help because participation was limited to answering direct questions during the morning session of the workshop.

Q: What could the trainer have done differently to avoid problem behavior?

A: The trainer could have conducted activities other than using direct questions and broken up a lecture with the discussion of other questions. Getting feedback from learners who are discussing ideas about taking orders over the telephone would avoid problem behaviors later in the day.

Q: What do you recommend the trainer do differently?

A: Next time, the trainer can ask learners questions about the organization's policies and procedures and discuss situations that commonly occur. Conduct activities that provide feedback that the new employees are learning. Give the learners a quiz before going to the lab. A quiz can even be in the form a crossword puzzle or a quiz show game. Providing an overview and objectives for a lab session helps learners identify what they will learn. Have the learners practice each part of the process prior to putting all the pieces of the process together.

Q: How can you apply the adult learning principles developed here to your training sessions?

A: The adult learning principles here are participation, practice, giving an overview of a lab session, and getting feedback. Learners can identify how they can improve in each of these areas.

ADULT LEARNING PRACTICE CASE STUDY 8

Security First

Directions: First, read the eighteen adult learning principles that follow. Then, read the situation following the adult learning principles, and identify what's wrong with this training session and identify which of the eighteen adult learning principles have been violated. Offer recommendations or suggestions to improve the class while honoring adult learning principles.

ADULT LEARNING PRINCIPLES

Following are eighteen adult learning principles. Be sure to honor the principles in adult learning situations that apply in a specific organization. These principles are not equally important. Their application depends on the context and situation in an organization.

Adult Motivation and Retention

1. Adults prefer to determine their **own** learning experiences.
2. Adults are motivated to learn when **they** identify they have a need to learn.
3. Adults are motivated by **societal or professional pressures,** which require a particular learning need.
4. Adults can be motivated to learn when the **benefits** of a learning experience outweigh the learner's resistance.
5. Adults use their knowledge from years of experience as a filter for new information and **don't change readily.**
6. Adults learn best from their own **experiences.**
7. An adult's experience is a filter that can function as a **catalyst or barrier** to learning something new.

8. Ninety percent of what adults learn and retain in long-term memory is tied to previous knowledge.
9. Adults like tangible **rewards and benefits** from training.

Adult Methods of Training

10. Some adults like **some lectures**. All adults won't like all lectures.
11. Adults like **small group discussion**.
12. Adults enjoy **practical** problem solving. Adults want **practical** answers for today's problems.
13. Adults retain learning that they **discover** and forget much of what they are told.
14. **Practice** is a part of the learning process, not the result of it.
15. **Assess**, don't assume.

Adult Classroom/Learning Environment

16. Adults hate to have their **time** wasted.
17. Adults like **physical** comfort.
18. Refreshments and breaks establish a **relaxed atmosphere** and convey **respect** to the learner.

CASE STUDY

The "New System Security" half-day training session begins with the instructor asking the class to form small groups and brainstorm their funniest memory as a software security technician. As the groups report, different awkward situations are acknowledged with the assurance that answers can be found in today's class to avoid these situations in the future. Then, one person in each group is asked to come to the front of the room to gather name tent materials, marker pens, picture magazines, glue, scissors, and other materials. Each person makes his or her own name tent that is symbolic of what he or she hopes to learn during the workshop. Individual objectives are shared within each group.

Each group is to come up with a team/group name and make a collage of common issues/problems faced by security technicians. Groups then report on their work product and share their insights about common problems. The instructor charts all of the group objectives on a flip chart. These introductory activities consume the first ninety minutes of the workshop. Participants are eager to get into the material, but it's time for the break.

- What's wrong here?
- Which adult learning principles (see the next page) are violated here?
- What recommendations or suggestions do you have to revise activities during the first ninety minutes of this class?

Facilitator Notes for Case Study 8

LEARNING OBJECTIVE: Given a case study, the learner will be able to identify how to use adult learning principles in climate setting activities.

Possible Case Answers

What's wrong here?

- Inappropriate use of the first ninety minutes through minimally beneficial activities.
- Three different climate-setting activities conducted when one would suffice.
- Introductory activities consumed ninety minutes and had little substance related to the technical content of the class.

Which adult learning principles (see the page before the case study) are violated here?

- (4) Adults can be motivated to learn when the benefits of a learning experience outweigh the learner's resistance.
- (5, 6, 7) Adults learn best from their own experiences. Having adults brainstorm funny memories does not honor the adult's experience about software security.
- (12) Adults enjoy practical problem solving. Adults want practical answers for today's problems.
- (16) Adults hate to have their time wasted.

What recommendations or suggestions do you have to revise activities during the first ninety minutes of this class?

- Select one climate-setting activity that is low risk, related to the content that follows, and involves everyone.
- Since this is a technical training class, avoid techniques that work better in "soft skills" training, like making collages and symbolic name tents.
- Select a problem-solving approach after having the software security technicians brainstorm issues.

Facilitator Processing Questions and Potential Answers

Q: Look at the eighteen adult learning principles on the page following this case study and circle those that are appropriate for your training situation.

Q: Select one or two of the circled principles and identify how you will honor each principle in your training.

A: There are no specific right answers to this activity. Participants can explain why these principles are important for their setting.

ADULT LEARNING APPLICATION CASE STUDY 9

Refresher Training

Directions: While reading this case study, identify whether the following ten adult learning skills used by a trainer are missing. If they are present, identify how well the skills are used by the trainer and recommend what can be done differently to improve the training session.

TEN ADULT LEARNING SKILLS FOR TRAINERS

1. Encourages learners to determine their own learning experiences.
2. Asks the learners to relate past experiences to learn something new.
3. Recognizes that adults use their knowledge from years of experience as a filter for new information and don't change readily.
4. Helps learners identify they have a need to learn.
5. Gives practical answers for today's problems.
6. Uses practical problem-solving techniques.
7. Uses teaching techniques that include learner participation, at least fifty percent of class time.
8. Helps learners identify the benefits and tangible rewards of training.
9. Avoids wasting the learners' time.
10. Provides for physical comfort with refreshments and breaks in a relaxed atmosphere.

CASE STUDY

The trainer began the "Refresher Customer Service" workshop by asking the Customer Service Representatives (CSRs), who had been with the telephone mail order catalog company for at least two years, to share two customer order stories with a partner: Tell one story about an order that had gone well and another about an order that had not gone well. Each person was allowed two minutes to tell both stories. At the end of four minutes the trainer attempted to bring the group back together and had to allow another five minutes for everyone to finish telling their stories. While stories were being finished, some learners left their seats to get coffee from the break room and a few latecomers were asked to find open seats and wait for the next activity.

In a large group discussion, the trainer then collected the stories of customer orders that had not gone well and asked the group to add other customer problems to the list, which became the agenda for the workshop. The trainer said, "This refresher workshop is like spring training for baseball players. Everyone needs to revisit the basics from time to time and brush up on skills they may have forgotten or not used often enough. The company's goal is continuous improvement; so let's begin to work on some of these difficult situations."

Each small group was assigned a customer problem situation and was asked to brainstorm suggestions on how to handle that situation more appropriately. The trainer pointed out posters of the telephone order process and trouble-shooting flowchart that are posted in the classroom as reference.

After each group reported on how to solve some of the customer problems, the trainer asked the rest of the class to use the telephone order process poster and trouble-shooting flowchart as a guide to critique each report. The first group was surprised by the critique and didn't understand that they were to use the poster and flowchart as part of their discussion. Other groups began side conversations to revise their reports.

After all the reports were finished, the trainer asked each participant to complete an action plan to describe what they will do differently when handling difficult customer order situations. The trainer provided copies of the telephone order process poster and trouble-shooting flowchart to each participant before ending the workshop.

- Which of the ten adult learning skills are missing?
- If they are present, identify how well the trainer used these skills.
- Recommend what can be done differently to improve the training session.

Facilitator Notes for Case Study 9

LEARNING OBJECTIVE: Given a case study and list of ten adult learning skills, identify which are present and which are missing. Make recommendations to improve the application of the ten adult learning principles.

Possible Case Answers

Which of the ten adult learning skills are missing?

- (4) "Helps learners identify they have a need to learn." The CSRs are forced to attend the training as part of a continuous improvement process.
- (7) "Uses teaching techniques that include learner participation, at least fifty percent of class time" is partially missing. Although learners told stories and brainstormed solutions to customer service problems, not enough time was allowed for these activities.
- (9) "Avoids wasting the learners' time" is partially missing. Because the instructor gave poor directions, learners didn't understand the problem solving brainstorming was intended to follow the two guides posted in the room (telephone order process poster and troubleshooting flowchart). Initial discussions wasted time because they did not use these two guides. Giving participants copies of these two guides during the training program, not at the end, would have helped learners follow directions.

If they are present, identify how well the trainer used these skills.

- (1) "Encourages learners to determine their own learning experiences."
- (2) "Asks the learners to relate past experiences to learn something new."
- (6) "Uses practical problem-solving techniques."

Recommend what can be done differently to improve the training session.

- Provide the two guides during the training.
- Allow enough time for learners to finish discussions.
- Have learners prioritize problems raised by the two stories.
- Tell the learners the purpose of the two stories, since only stories about poor customer service situations were used later in the workshop.
- Check with the learners to identify whether the spring training analogy has meaning for this target population. Also, check with the learners and identify whether a refresher is appropriate.

Facilitator Processing Questions and Potential Answers

Q: Which of the ten adult learning skills are most critical to the success of the workshop presented in the case study? Why?

A: For experienced CSRs, skill 3, "recognizes that adults use their knowledge from years of experience as a filter for new information and don't change readily" is a key skill. The trainer in the case study did build the lesson on the past experiences of the CSRs. Skill 5 is important, since it was the learners, not the trainer who identified what problems the group would discuss and solve.

Q: Which of the ten adult learning skills do you need to work on? How will you do that?

A: Answers to this question will depend on the needs of individual participants.

Adult Learning Serial Case Study

Each of the four types of case studies in this chapter deals with adult learning skills. When used in the same workshop, they build on one another, so learners progress in their ability to diagnose, problem solve, practice, and apply the learnings from cases. Use the facilitator processing questions below to combine all four of the case studies as a serial case study.

Facilitator Processing Questions and Potential Answers

Q: What have you learned about adult learning principles that are most important when adapting these principles to your situation?

Q: What problems can you overcome by honoring adult learning principles in your situation?

Q: What are you likely to do differently during your next training session to avoid the problems seen in the previous "adult learning" case studies?

A: Answers to these questions above will be personalized to individual training situations.

5

Assertion Case Studies

THIS CHAPTER contains five types of case studies that teach various lessons about three behavior styles: assertive, non-assertive, and aggressive. Case studies are intended to help learners act more assertively and discourage the use of non-assertive and aggressive behavior in others. Different case studies in this chapter might be used in "communication," "conflict resolution," or "management development" workshops.

See the Introduction to Part 2 on pages 63–64 for suggestions on how to select and customize the case studies in this chapter.

ASSERTION IDENTIFICATION CASE STUDY 10

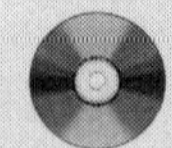

How Do You Feel?

Directions: For each situation,

- *Identify the other character's behavior as assertive, non-assertive, or aggressive.*
- *Decide if you are being placed in a position that requires either initiative from you or a response to another person. For example, "initiative" is taking the first step, such as, introducing yourself to someone you don't know. A "response" is waiting for someone else to introduce you to others or waiting for others to introduce themselves to you.*

---

1. At work, another support person asked you to donate money for a gift for a co-worker. You calmly and politely decline. Now she is berating you, in front of others, for being cheap, stingy, and selfish.
2. You are busy at work when an angry manager comes in, screams at you, and calls you stupid and incompetent. He says you made an error that you know nothing about.
3. One of your co-workers is a true know-it-all and is frequently right. Today you need to use the new word processing package to do an especially important document. She is the expert on the new system (as she is quick to point out to all) and you could really use her help.
4. You have a major report to finish today. It will require at least an hour of uninterrupted time. You are planning to negotiate with the other support person to answer your phone lines for about an hour. This is not an uncommon arrangement in your department. Your concern is that she will agree to anything you ask—very pleasantly—but then she may let you down just when you need help.
5. You are in charge of the department Christmas party this year. Plans are about set and you are telling the group what you've done. One of your co-workers, as

usual, begins picking the plans apart: "That won't work." "It's too much money." "No one will come." . . . and so on.

6. The office has become intolerably overcrowded with both people and "stuff." Several of you have approached the boss with ideas about rearranging the area. Storage space is available and there are even a couple of areas down the hall that could become another workspace. The boss is supportive and recognizes there is a problem, but no action! He can't seem to make a decision.
7. You've had several great ideas lately that have helped cut down on some tedious and repetitious tasks in the office. Today you overheard the office manager telling the Director how *she* had streamlined the office procedures and saved huge amounts of time and money.
8. One of your co-workers in your area complains about everything from the workload to the office temperature. Today she has been especially vocal about some of the new personnel policies. Yesterday she complained at length about the boss. The day before it was her kids.

Facilitator Notes for Case Study 10

LEARNING OBJECTIVE: Given a case study, identify whether another person's behavior is aggressive or non-assertive and requires initiative or a response to handle assertively.

Possible Case Answers

1. The other person's behavior is aggressive and requires a response from you.
2. The other person's behavior is aggressive and requires a response from you.
3. The other person's behavior typically is aggressive and requires initiative from you.
4. The other person's behavior is aggressive and requires initiative from you.
5. The other person's behavior is critical, maybe aggressive and requires a response from you.
6. The other person's behavior is non-assertive and requires initiative from you.
7. The other person's behavior is aggressive and requires initiative from you.
8. The other person's behavior is non-assertive since she refuses to do more than complain and requires a response from you.

Facilitator Processing Questions and Potential Answers

Q: What are the characteristics of aggressive behavior, assertive behavior, and non-assertive behavior?

A: Characteristics of aggressive, assertive, and non-assertive behaviors are

Aggressive behavior:

- Others have to lose in order to win
- Put down or control others
- Blame others for poor results
- Righteous, competitive, opinionated, defensive, and accusing

Assertive behavior:

- Influence is shared, respects self and others
- Responsible for own behavior, feelings, beliefs
- Expressive, listens, candid, diplomatic, empathic, self-confident

Non-assertive behavior:

- Appeasing others
- Blames self for poor results
- Others are responsible for how they feel
- Victim, whining, apologetic, passive, guilty, hurt, anxious
- Has difficulty saying "no" to unreasonable requests

Q: Which of the three types of behavior is most difficult for you to deal with?

A: Answers will vary.

Q: Is it easier for you to deal with aggressive and non-assertive behavior when initiating the communication (asking for help, making introductions, etc.); or is it easier for you to deal with aggressive and non-assertive behavior when responding to the other person (answering complaints, responding to an angry customer or supervisor, etc.)?

A: Answers will vary.

ASSERTION PROBLEM SOLVING CASE STUDY 11

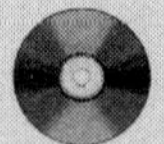

Customer Is Calling

Directions: Identify the problems caused by the aggressive and non-assertive behavior in this case. Recommend at least two actions the manager can take to solve these problems.

The administrative support person is out for the third day in a row on jury duty. Several phone lines are on hold, and staff members are blaming each other for not pitching in to cover all the calls. One staff member has complained to the manager that the phone system is inadequate when the administrative support person is absent. The manager recalls having heard this complaint before, but is concerned about exceeding his department budget by buying a new phone system or hiring temporary help.

Department mail has not been sorted or delivered. Different staff members have gone through the mail and retrieved their own correspondence. Phone messages for staff members are not in the usual central location, and customers are complaining that their requests from three days ago are unanswered.

Phone calls slowed down a bit during the lunch hour, so the manager told everyone to take a lunch break while he alone covered the phones. During the lunch hour, some calls were unanswered. One of the unanswered calls was from a large account that is waiting for a persistent delivery issue to be resolved. This customer left a message to cancel all their orders; he would buy from a competitor where he could get better service.

Facilitator Notes for Case Study 11

LEARNING OBJECTIVE: Given a case study, identify the problems caused by aggressive and non-assertive behavior and recommend at least two actions the manager can take to solve these problems.

Possible Case Answers

These are some of the problems caused by aggressive and non-assertive behavior:

1. No one has taken over the screening of department phone calls, sorting mail, and taking messages. Staff members are behaving aggressively and blaming others.
2. The manager has allowed personnel and budget problems to impact the efficiency of the department and they are losing customers and one large account. The manager's non-assertive behavior and indecisiveness seems to have caused some of these problems.

Suggested actions for the manager:

1. Assign a substitute to screen calls, take messages, and sort mail.
2. Assign staff members rotating responsibility to cover the phone during the lunch hour.
3. Research the cost of a new or enhanced phone system that could address the volume of calls and unanswered calls.
4. Discuss staffing needs with the Director of Human Resources and the manager's Director.

Facilitator Processing Questions and Potential Answers

Q: What is the relationship between workflow problems and non-assertive behavior?

A: When problems go unidentified or are not addressed, they can become worse. Rarely do problems diminish or disappear by ignoring them.

Q: What types of problems often arise through indecision by managers?

A: The types of problems that often arise through indecision range from simple to complex and often get more complicated as time goes on. In this case, what started out as a phone coverage problem turned into losing a major account.

Q: What types of issues are you facing that cause procrastination or indecision? What can you do about them?

A: Answers will vary depending on the types of issues raised by the participants.

ASSERTION PRACTICE CASE STUDIES 12 AND 13

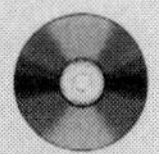

Directions: The assertion skills being practiced in the two case studies that follow are for employees to respond to a challenging situation by speaking assertively. Prior to reading the case studies, the learners need to see a model of assertive responses. The model suggested here is "DESC Scripting."[1] DESC stands for a script that:

"D" describes the other person's behavior that you see or hear.

"E" express your feelings or explain the consequences of the other person's behavior.

"S" specify a change of behavior you want the other person to make.

"C" consequences (positive if the behavior is changed and/or negative if the behavior is not changed).

Case 12: She's All I Need Right Now

The staff support person who usually works on your floor is absent because of illness and a replacement is here today. It has been a hectic morning. Work is piling up faster than you can get to it. At the moment, the replacement support person is angry because one of the requisitions doesn't have a number on it. She is muttering under her breath, pushing papers around, and acting generally ugly. She has told anyone who happens to be listening how inefficient this department is, saying, "Obviously, the rest of you here don't know what you're doing."

Plan a script for responding assertively to this aggressive behavior:

- Describe
- Express or explain
- Specify
- Choose the consequences

[1]Adapted from Sharon Anthony Bower and Gordon H. Bower, "Asserting Yourself" published by Addison Wesley © 1976.

Case 13: Her Kids Call All the Time

One of the employees in your department is a single parent with three school-age children at home. They call her constantly during work. Not just for emergencies, but to mediate their arguments and to "tattle" on each other. She has been counseled twice about the calls, but since you and she are new friends she counts on you to help her with this situation. The time you spend trying to find her takes you away from your work and the calls add significantly to the interruptions in your already chaotic day. The time has come to deal with this conflict.

Plan a script for responding assertively to this non-assertive behavior:

- Describe
- Express or explain
- Specify
- Choose the consequences

Facilitator Notes for Case Studies 12 and 13

LEARNING OBJECTIVE: Given two case studies, write a DESC script to respond assertively to each person's aggressive or non-assertive behavior.

Possible Case Answers

Here are suggested DESC scripts for the two Practice Case Studies:

12. This script is in response to the aggressive behavior of the other employee. [Describe] When you find requisitions that are in some way incomplete, [explain] I'm concerned that we need to correct them. [Specify] If you would tell me directly what the problem is [consequence], then the work can be completed more efficiently.
13. This script is in response to the non-assertive behavior of the other employee. [Describe] When you are away from your desk and your children call, [explain] it takes me away from my work to find you. [Specify] I would prefer to take a message and have you return personal calls when you return to your desk, [consequences] that way I won't have so many interruptions.

Facilitator Processing Questions and Potential Answers

Q: Which of these scripts was most difficult to deal with? What made it difficult?

A: This answer will vary with each participant. Be sure learners provide a rationale for an answer.

Q: What makes a good DESC script?

A: A good DESC script follows the formula, is brief and considerate of the person hearing the script.

Q: What is a situation you face where a DESC script would be appropriate? Write that script.

A: This answer will vary for each participant. Use the DESC script formula to evaluate answers.

ASSERTION APPLICATION CASE STUDIES 14, 15, 16

During a workshop on "How to Conduct a Performance Appraisal," supervisors and managers were taught a variety of techniques to handle non-assertive and aggressive behavior of subordinate employees. The strategies are summarized below. The managers and supervisors were then asked to apply the strategies in three difficult situations about assertively discussing differences of opinion.

Behavior Styles to Handle Differences

Below are non-assertive and aggressive behavior styles exhibited by some employees during a Performance Appraisal discussion. Specific strategies are shown for supervisors and managers to handle the different styles during an appraisal discussion.

Non-Assertive Style	Strategy
1. Employee takes information personally.	1. Give specific examples of behavior. Separate the behavior from the person. "I'm concerned with what you did/didn't do. Let's focus on what you can *do* to be more successful."
2. Employee seeks external validation, he or she really wants the supervisor's approval.	2. Have the employee complete a self-appraisal. Ask for this employee's opinion more often. Ask more questions and give fewer answers.
3. Employee feels he or she needs to take the blame for things that have gone wrong.	3. Focus on results and outcomes, not blame. Identify what needs to be done differently and this employee's contribution to reaching the goal.
4. Employee apologizes excessively and over-promises; finds it difficult to say no or negotiate duties/tasks.	4. Be realistic in your expectations and time limits to complete tasks. Be specific in making requests.

5. Employee is silent, does not share reaction to your ratings, and is passive in goal setting.	5. Be sure the employee completes the self-appraisal prior to meeting with you. If necessary, return the self-appraisal for more preparation by the employee. Use basic and follow-up questions until you get an answer.
6. Employee does not want to take on new challenges or set "stretch" goals, he or she prefers to be safe with known tasks.	6. Focus on the possible, ask for small steps, set limited and specific smaller goals.
Aggressive Style	**Strategy**
1. Employee challenges your ratings and perceptions, even argues with you over small points, and has difficulty listening to criticism.	1. Be specific in describing observed behaviors. Use "acknowledging" skills to agree with facts and how the employee feels.
2. Employee blames others for his/her shortcomings, even covers up mistakes.	2. Focus on what needs to be done differently, rather than fixing blame.
3. Employee interrupts you when he/she hears a "trigger" word and does not listen to your full comment.	3. Be aware of what words may trigger a reaction from the employee. Ask the employee to give you a chance to finish your entire comment.
4. Employee offers several points together, making it difficult to respond to each point.	4. Ask the employee to slow down so you can keep track of each point. Write down each point if necessary and respond to each one.
5. Employee claims your rating is inconsistent with past ratings . . . why the change now?	5. Acknowledge the employee has a point and state you are aware this is a change in the appraisal system.

6. Employee continues to go back to the same point that you have covered at least once or twice already during the discussion.	6. Be firm and repeat your stance. Clarify any confusion and move on.
7. Employee compares his or her performance as better than co-workers and asks how you rated other employees.	7. Tell the employee you are conducting his or her appraisal based on his or her performance against goals and not comparing performance to others. Information about how others are rated is confidential.
8. Employee claims to be speaking for himself or herself and co-workers when making a statement of opinion.	8. Ask the employee to speak only for himself or herself. You will/did have conversations with others individually.

CASE STUDIES

Directions: Use the strategies or skills on the previous pages to handle the differences described in the case study, and answer the three questions for each case study that follows:

1. *Why is it difficult to respond to this subordinate?*
2. *What is your usual pattern of response?*
3. *What is an assertive response?*

Case 14: Staying in Control

During a Performance Appraisal interview, your subordinate, who is a very senior person, seems one step ahead of all your questions and discussion points. He has done a great job in completing a self-appraisal. As a matter of fact, you have reworded some comments on your form to use his words in place of yours. You are now discussing "New Goals" for the next appraisal period. Your subordinate has written and presented you with five goals that concern one aspect of his job. The goals are not challenging and can easily be achieved in a few months.

You want to focus on other areas of his job that are more challenging and will also require him to move into new areas of responsibility and will take longer than three months to accomplish. He is somewhat uncomfortable in this new area because he lacks skills and needs training that less senior people have already accomplished. You begin to talk about this new area of responsibility and he ignores your questions and comments by again talking about the goals that he has written.

1. Why is it difficult to respond to this subordinate?
2. What is your usual pattern of response?
3. What is an assertive response?

Case 15: Resolving Differences

You are conducting a Performance Appraisal interview with your subordinate, who is an intelligent and enthusiastic junior person in the department. He has rated all behaviors under the ten "Personal Skills Appraisal" dimensions as "Exceeds Requirements" ("E") or "Meets Requirements" ("M").

You have rated six of the ten behaviors as "Needs Improvement" ("N"), including "*listens with concentration.*" As soon as he sees your form, he explodes and accuses you of being unfair and "always picking on him because he is the newest person in the department."

1. Why is it difficult to respond to this subordinate?
2. What is your usual pattern of response?
3. What is an assertive response?

Case 16: Unresolved Differences

You are conducting a Performance Appraisal interview with your subordinate, who is an experienced person but who has been in your group only eight months. Your observations during the last few months are starting to reveal that her experience is limited to a few areas.

Your rating of her *Job Knowledge* is a combination of "M" and one "E" rating. In her self-appraisal, she has rated herself with all "E's." After discussing this difference for about 15 minutes, she has not altered her ratings and strongly disagrees with your "M" ratings.

1. Why is it difficult to respond to this subordinate?
2. What is your usual pattern of response?
3. What is an assertive response?

Facilitator Notes for Case Studies 14, 15, 16

LEARNING OBJECTIVE: Given three case studies about handling differences during a performance appraisal discussion, use the fourteen strategies appropriately.

Possible Case Answers

When facing differences of opinion during a performance review discussion, six strategies for assertively responding to a non-assertive employee and eight strategies for assertively responding to an aggressive employee were offered. In the three case studies, participants are asked to apply those strategies while answering three questions:

1. Why is it difficult to respond to this subordinate?
2. What is your usual pattern of response?
3. What is an assertive response?

Case 14: Staying in Control

1. Why is it difficult to respond to this subordinate? It is difficult to respond to this subordinate since this is a skilled and very senior person. He prefers to work on easier and shorter-term projects.
2. What is your usual pattern of response? A usual pattern of response would be a personal answer.
3. What is an assertive response? The aggressive style of his response is identified in items 1 and 6. His response is also an example of the non-assertive style in item 6. He is not listening and goes back to his points. Acknowledge the facts and how the employee feels, such as, "I know learning new skills is somewhat uncomfortable." Be firm about talking about new goals, restate your question, and ask for a specific answer before moving to another point. Ask the

employee to focus on specific small and limited steps to begin to work on the goals that are more difficult and challenging.

Case 15: Resolving Differences

1. Why is it difficult to respond to this subordinate? This situation is difficult because the new person explodes and becomes defensive and suggests you are picking on him.
2. What is your usual pattern of response? A usual pattern of response would be a personal answer.
3. What is an assertive response? The aggressive style of his response is identified in items 1 and 7. Acknowledge facts and how the employee feels. Give specific examples to back up the "Needs Improvement" ratings. Tell the employee you are not picking on him. If the employee has difficulty calming down, end the session and make an appointment to finish the discussion at a later time.

Case 16: Unresolved Differences

1. Why is it difficult to respond to this subordinate? The aggressive style of her response is identified in items 1 and 7. She also might feel a bit insecure about her lack of broader experience.
2. What is your usual pattern of response? A usual pattern of response would be a personal answer.
3. What is an assertive response? Acknowledge facts and feelings. Give specific examples of lack of experience and why you are focusing on the broader job, not just the part of her experience. Find areas of agreement to build upon. Tell her what she can do to be rated higher next time. You may have to agree to disagree and not reach consensus. After all, this is the supervisor's opinion and rating of the employee's performance. In many organizations, you may submit a different opinion and have it filed with the Performance Appraisal.

Facilitator Processing Questions and Potential Answers

Q: What did you learn about using different strategies for dealing with non-assertive and aggressive responses to employees who have a different opinion in a performance appraisal discussion?

Q: Which of the strategies seem easier for you to implement?

Q: What would help you use these strategies more effectively?

A: Answers to these questions are likely to be individualized.

ASSERTION SERIAL CASE STUDY 17

Directions: The following are three progressive situations that occur to the same employee who is having his or her performance reviewed by the same manager. The employee needs to handle differences with the manager assertively. Answer the three questions at the end of each case.

1. *Why is it difficult to respond to your manager in this situation?*
2. *What is your usual pattern of response?*
3. *What is an assertive response?*

Situation 1: No Good Deed Goes Unpunished

Your manager has been encouraging you to take on more responsibility. You have taken on several special projects during the last year and are busier than others in your department. During your Performance Planning discussion, your manager asks you to take on work that another person used to do. That other person is no longer with the company. The job needs to get done, but you don't think you have the skill or the knowledge to take on an additional responsibility in addition to the "full plate" you already have.

1. Why is it difficult to respond to your manager in this situation?
2. What is your usual pattern of response?
3. What is an assertive response?

Situation 2: A Difference of Opinion

As part of the performance planning process, your manager asked you to complete a self-appraisal. Now that you are sitting with your manager having the performance planning discussion, you realize that your manager rated your performance significantly different than you did in several areas. You rated yourself a "4" or "5" on acquiring six core competencies and completing one performance objective. Your manager rated you a "3" on the same items. When you ask for clarification your manager gets defensive and accuses you of "not seeing the big picture."

1. Why is it difficult to respond to your manager in this situation?
2. What is your usual pattern of response?
3. What is an assertive response?

Situation 3: Don't You Remember?

You have contributed to a plan to improve the workflow in your department. During the performance planning discussion with your manager, your contribution seems to have been forgotten by everyone. You are not receiving credit for your ideas and accomplishments.

1. Why is it difficult to respond to your manager in this situation?
2. What is your usual pattern of response?
3. What is an assertive response?

Facilitator Notes for Case Study 17

LEARNING OBJECTIVE: Given three situations, select the appropriate assertive strategy for dealing with progressively difficult situations.

Possible Case Answers

The three situations are about the same person who needs to assertively confront three different issues during the same performance review discussion. In the three situations, participants are asked:

1. Why is it difficult to respond to your manager in this situation?
2. What is your usual pattern of response?
3. What is an assertive response?

Situation 1: No Good Deed Goes Unpunished

1. It is difficult to respond because you are being asked to do more work than other employees and you are not sure you have the knowledge or skill for added responsibilities. You already have too much to do.
2. A usual pattern of response would be a personal answer.
3. An assertive response would be to identify what is possible to do and to ask your manager for additional training. Also ask if there are tasks that others can do so you can have the time to learn and do new tasks.

Situation 2: A Difference of Opinion

1. It is difficult to respond because there is a difference of opinion and when you ask for clarification your manager gets defensive and accusatory.

2. A usual pattern of response would be a personal answer.
3. An assertive response would be to acknowledge areas of agreement and that you have a different view of your performance. Ask for clarification about what the big picture looks like and how your responsibilities fit into the big picture.

Situation 3: Don't You Remember?

1. This is a difficult situation because your ideas seem to be forgotten and to remind your manager of your accomplishments might be seen as boastful.
2. A usual pattern of response would be a personal answer.
3. An assertive response would be to remind your manager of the workflow improvement you contributed and ask that it be listed as an accomplishment.

Facilitator Processing Questions and Potential Answers

Q: What did you learn about using different strategies for dealing with non-assertive and aggressive responses with someone who has a different opinion in a performance appraisal discussion?

Q: Which of the strategies seem easier for you to implement?

Q: What would help you use these strategies more effectively?

A: Answers to these questions are likely to be individualized.

6

Change Management

THIS CHAPTER contains five types of case studies that teach various lessons about how supervisors and managers can implement changes, reduce employee resistance to changes, and gain support for changes that occur in any organization. Case studies in this chapter might be used in "change management" or "conflict resolution" workshops.

See the Introduction to Part 2 on pages 63–64 for suggestions on how to select and customize the case studies in this chapter.

CHANGE MANAGEMENT IDENTIFICATION CASE STUDIES 18 AND 19

The model below shows nine stages in responding to the news of a change. There are several models of the change process. This model loosely parallels Elisabeth Kubler-Ross's model of grieving from her book *On Death and Dying*. Individuals often deny that a change is happening and then become fearful of what will happen to them when the change occurs. The concern can be for job security, capabilities, and loss of prestige among peers. Fear or worry often turns to anger at having a change forced upon employees and frustration with not being consulted about how or why a change is to be made. Anger often turns to sadness where employees recall how wonderful their world was in the "good ole days" and how sad it is that all these terrible changes have occurred.

Some employees eventually realize that the change is not going away and accept it and begin to adjust to the new way. Some employees eventually realize that some aspects of their job are actually better and it is a relief to be rid of some of the older ways that got in the way of their success. Then employees are able to find the new way interesting, and even like and enjoy the new way.

During a workshop on managing change and the resistance that accompanies many changes, it is helpful for employees to recognize where they are in the process of change and how to move forward in the process to the next stage. If a stage is missed or gone through quickly, employees often need to return to the missed or skipped stage so they can take care of unfinished business. Employees often regress and go through various stages several times before moving beyond acceptance (considered a neutral stage) to the positive side of the model. Managers who attempt to pull or push an employee through the stages of change are often unsuccessful. Non-supportive or pushy behavior can cause an employee to get stuck in a stage or regress.

For supervisors to help employees move through the stages of change, first they must recognize the stage where an employee is in order to help that person to move forward. See Figure 6.1 for the Nine Stages of Change Model.

Figure 6.1. Nine Stages of Change Model.

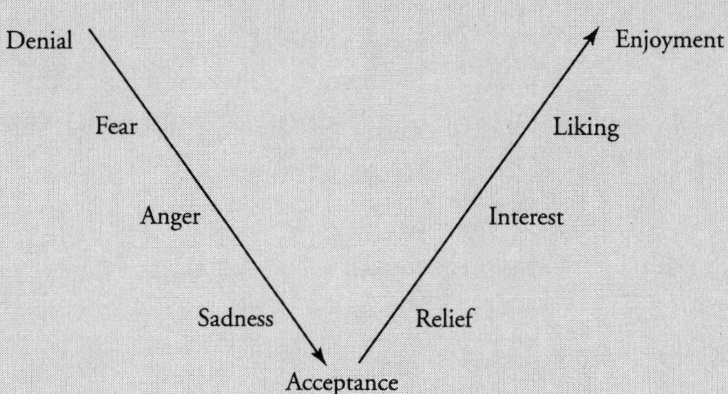

OVERCOMING RESISTANCE TO CHANGE

Directions: Here are two case studies about employees who are resisting a change. As you read the cases, identify where the employee is in the nine stages of change (Figure 6.1), and why it is difficult for the employee and the supervisor to deal with this situation.

Case 18: New Workflow Process

The supervisor is attempting to show the employee how new job duties fit into a redesigned workflow process. The employee says to the supervisor "I can't believe you want us to go along with these changes. This must be a mistake. And besides, it's not my job to do other people's work." The employee further complains about several old issues the supervisor thought were solved long ago.

1. What is the stage of resistance for the employee?
2. Why is it difficult for the employee to deal with this situation?
3. Why is it difficult for the supervisor to deal with this situation?

Case 19: Support Person

After learning completely new tasks, the Support Person's mistakes are piling up faster than they can be cleared. The Support Person doesn't feel she has complete directions for these new tasks. She has asked for help in clearing the mistakes and comments, "Things have really changed around here. It's not like the old days when everyone knew what they were doing." Up until now, her supervisor has used positive reinforcement techniques and tells the Support Person that she is pleased with how hard she is trying to do her job. She assures the confused Support Person that everything will work out just fine.

1. What is the stage of resistance for the employee?
2. Why is it difficult for the employee to deal with this situation?
3. Why is it difficult for the supervisor to deal with this situation?

Facilitator Notes for Case Studies 18 and 19

LEARNING OBJECTIVE: Given a model for the nine stages of change and two case studies, identify the correct stage of resistance for the employee and the difficulties of addressing the situation appropriately.

Possible Case Answers

Case 18: New Workflow Process

1. What is the stage of resistance for the employee? The employee is in denial.
2. Why is it difficult for the employee to deal with this situation? The employee has gotten stuck on several past, unresolved issues.
3. Why is it difficult for the supervisor to deal with this situation? The supervisor has not paid attention to the employee's past complaints and perhaps sees this employee as a chronic complainer. The supervisor seems to assume everything is O.K. in spite of the complaints.

Case 19: Support Person

1. What is the stage of resistance for the employee? The employee is stuck in "sadness" and seems to long for the good ole days.
2. Why is it difficult for the employee to deal with this situation? The employee does not know how to do the tasks and has asked for help in correcting mistakes. She isn't getting any help, so the situation probably won't get better by itself.
3. Why is it difficult for the supervisor to deal with this situation? The supervisor is in "denial" since she keeps reinforcing mistakes, rather than providing skills training for the support person.

Facilitator Processing Questions and Potential Answers

Q: Why was it easy or difficult for you to identify in which of the nine stages the person might be in?

A: Individual answers may vary depending on a person's understanding of the nine stages.

Q: Why is it difficult for some employees to deal with change?

A: Individual answers may very depending on personal experience.

Q: What can you do to help yourself move to the next stage of change?

A: To move from one stage of change to the next, use the ten strategies listed with the "Skill Practice Case Studies" in this chapter.

CHANGE MANAGEMENT PROBLEM SOLVING CASE STUDY 20

Merger Mania

Directions: The following are five suggestions for managers and supervisors who are contemplating a change, and how to reduce the level of resistance to the intended changes.

1. *Share the need for the change before initiating it.*
2. *Describe the benefits and issues about the reasons for the change.*
3. *Ask employees to participate in the planning for the change. Solicit and use their suggestions.*
4. *Implement the changes in gradual phases.*
5. *Assess the results and develop alternatives for unexpected consequences of the changes.*

Identify what problems may occur when two firms are about to merge. What is the source of the problem? Consider which of the five suggestions above might be helpful in resolving some of these problems.

Two small medical malpractice law firms of nearly equal size are merging their practices. Many of the terms of the merger have been worked out. Some of the practical, administrative implementation issues have not been discussed. Neither firm has enough office space to house the new merged firm, so new office space needs to be found. One possible location is geographically midway between the two firms, which means about half of the employees in each firm will have a longer commute to work.

Although existing computers in each firm are networked, each firm has a different computer platform, and so one firm will need to convert its files and the employees will need to adapt to different software. The most senior administrative assistant says she isn't going to learn any new systems. After all, she is only a year from retirement. She has been with the firm since it began and has lots of case history in her memory along with the goodwill of every client.

The libraries of the two firms are almost identical. Surely it isn't necessary to have two sets of resource books. The two firms have different filing systems for closed cases. Worksheets and templates for the two firms are similar, but have substantial differences.

Questions:

1. What problems may occur when two firms merge?
2. What are the sources of the problems?
3. Which of the five suggestions above might be helpful in resolving some of these problems?

Facilitator Notes for Case Study 20

LEARNING OBJECTIVE: Given a case study, identify problems, the sources of the problems, and appropriate suggestions.

Possible Case Answers

1. What problems may occur when two firms merge? Most of the problems involve lack of planning around administrative issues:
   - Office space to accommodate the merged staffs
   - Longer commuting distances for some might not be equitable
   - Need for one computer platform and conversion of files into one network
   - Senior employee who doesn't want to learn a new system
   - Different filing systems for closed cases
   - Different worksheets and templates
2. What are the sources of the problems? Lack of planning around logistics and administrative issues seems to be a source along with not including senior administrative personnel in helping make these plans.
3. Which of the five suggestions mentioned in the directions might be helpful in resolving some of these problems? Suggestions 1 through 4 need to be developed prior to implementing changes and assessing results.

Facilitator Processing Questions and Potential Answers

Q: What types of problems seem to become bigger than necessary issues?

A: Issues that are ignored seem to become bigger problems.

Q: What can be done to avoid having these issues develop into problems?

A: To avoid these problems, plan for the change and use the five suggestions.

Q: Which of the five suggestions are appropriate to implement in your situation?

A: Answers will vary with the individual.

CHANGE MANAGEMENT PRACTICE CASE STUDIES 21 AND 22

Leaders Respond to Employee Resistance

Directions: Referencing the nine stages of change model presented during the "Diagnostic Case Study," supervisors can use these suggestions to help employees move from one stage of resisting change to the next. Employees can also use these suggestions to help themselves move to the next stage of change. Moving through stages of change is easier when you . . .

1. *Let go and say "good-bye" to the old habits and ways.*
2. *Shift to a new point of view to stay positive.*
3. *Have feelings of denial, fear, and anger acknowledged.*
4. *Have enough information and resources.*
5. *Understand the purpose of the change.*
6. *See the need for change and it makes sense.*
7. *Have input in the planning and execution of the change.*
8. *Feel a new skill can be learned and do not fear failure.*
9. *Are excited and energized by new projects that stretch abilities.*
10. *Don't spend time and energy getting frustrated with things you can't do anything about.*

Here are two case studies about supervisors who are trying to apply new skills when responding to an employee's resistance to change. As you read the cases, identify

- Where the employee is in the nine stages of change (see previous nine-step model earlier in this chapter)?
- Why is it difficult to deal with this situation?
- Which ten strategies above might be effective in this situation?

Case 21: It's Too Difficult!

An employee has been trained to complete her part of the new work process. The employee is having difficulty doing the task correctly and her work is being returned. The supervisor has sent detailed e-mail and voice mail messages to describe how the employee can correctly perform new job duties. The supervisor has described in great detail exactly how to complete each activity in the workflow process. The employee tells the supervisor by return e-mail that what she is expected to do is "too difficult," she "doesn't know how to do that," and is concerned about the consequences for clients if her efforts fail.

1. What is the stage of resistance for the employee?
2. What makes this situation difficult to deal with?
3. What strategies might help this situation?

Case 22: This Isn't Fair!

An employee has just learned how to complete a task and has received written instructions about additional changes in the workflow process. Changes have been rolling out faster than the employee can get used to them. The supervisor has not been willing to discuss the reasons behind the changes and suggests the employee just go along with each request. The supervisor tells the employee she doesn't know any more about the change than what is provided in the written directions. The employee is upset by this approach and says, "This isn't fair. How can they expect me to do a good job when they keep changing everything we do? If these people knew what it was like to do this job, they wouldn't be making these stupid suggestions!"

1. What is the stage of resistance for the employee?
2. What makes this situation difficult to deal with?
3. What strategies might help this situation?

Facilitator Notes for Case Studies 21 and 22

LEARNING OBJECTIVE: Given a case study, identify the stage of resistance for the employee and suggest a successful strategy to help the employee reduce resistance to the change.

Possible Case Answers

Case 21: It's Too Difficult!

1. What is the stage of resistance for the employee? The employee is at the "fear" stage.
2. What makes this situation difficult to deal with? The employee seems to be trying to do the task the new way correctly and is not successful. The supervisor so far has only offered detailed written directions, as opposed to offering a demonstration, or guided practice with feedback.
3. What strategies might help this situation? Perhaps the employee needs some encouragement, and face-to-face coaching would be helpful along with background information about why the changes are necessary.

Case 22: This Isn't Fair!

1. What is the stage of resistance for the employee? The employee is at the "anger" stage.
2. What makes this situation difficult to deal with? The supervisor doesn't know any more about the changes than the employee.
3. What strategies might help this situation?
   - Have feelings of denial, fear, and anger acknowledged.
   - Have enough information and resources.
   - Understand the purpose of the change.
   - See the need for change.

Facilitator Processing Questions and Potential Answers

Q: Which two or three of these ten strategies seems to be helpful in these situations?

A: Try providing more information, discuss the purpose of the change, and why the change is needed. Additional answers will vary with the individual.

Q: What are other strategies you can suggest that are not listed here?

A: The supervisor can discuss what consequences are for the client. Some additional answers will vary with the individual.

Q: What seems to make a *good* change strategy?

A: A good change strategy is positive and focused on one stage at a time. A good change strategy must acknowledge where someone is and helps move an individual to the next stage.

Q: Which strategies would be helpful for you in your situation?

A: Answers will vary with the individual.

CHANGE MANAGEMENT APPLICATION CASE STUDY 23

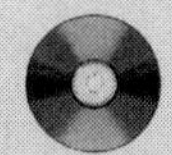

Change Is Never-Ending

Directions: Here is a summary of the skills taught in a change management workshop. Read these strategies, then apply them to the case that follows. Answer the questions at the end of the case study.

To take an active, supportive, leadership role in helping others transition through the stages of change, use these ten personal strategies to:

1. Find ways to help others let go and say "good-bye" to the old habits and ways.
2. Shift to a new point of view to stay positive and help others do the same.
3. Acknowledge feelings of denial, fear, and anger in yourself and others.
4. Provide enough information and resources.
5. Communicate the purpose of the change.
6. Share the need for change and how it makes sense.
7. Seek input in the planning and execution of the change.
8. Provide time and resources for new skill building and celebrate failures as well as successes.
9. Be excited and energized by new projects that stretch abilities.
10. Don't spend time and energy getting frustrated with things you can't do anything about.

Due to changes in federal and state social welfare law, employees at the county welfare office are experiencing several changes in how benefits are administered, and how duties and responsibilities are carried out. Some of the changes include:

- Using technology to verify recipient information and shorten the waiting time to receive benefits.
- Combining service delivery locations so employment, rent subsidies, general relief grants, food stamps, job skills training, and other benefits are available at one location.
- Changing the duties and responsibilities of employees to deliver more services, rather than specializing in one aspect of service delivery.
- Combining databases for all welfare recipients throughout the state.
- Social workers and other administrative employees need to learn to use new software to do their jobs.
- Social workers providing more job skills training and one-on-one counseling.
- Need for outplacement of county employees as welfare rolls decline.

Given these changes, here is a typical day for Barbara, a social worker who is in the midst of transition. Barbara now commutes to a newly opened satellite social service center by herself since she has just been transferred to a new office 15 miles further from home. She has yet to find a new car pool, so her commute to work is 30 minutes longer than before. Barbara used to be an "intake social worker" who interviewed new clients and screened them for benefits.

She has attended several meetings in the past month to learn about changes and identify additional new job responsibilities she will perform including making visits to clients' homes, giving job counseling, conducting basic work skills training sessions, and closing cases for clients who become employed. In the previous system, different social workers specialized in each of these areas. Now social workers will be assigned to individual clients and be the sole contact for all services. Barbara is concerned that her caseload of 75 recipients is too high while she is learning how to provide all the services a client needs.

Barbara has complained to her supervisor about her longer commute, constantly being away from her new responsibilities to attend technical and program training as well as being overwhelmed by her caseload. In the past ten years, the county has been in a constant state of change. Programs come and go. She is skeptical that any of these new changes will last very long before being replaced with the next wave of changes. Perhaps just keeping a low profile and doing the minimum required to survive all these changes is the best approach.

1. Why is it difficult for employees to deal with these types of change situations?
2. Which of the ten strategies mentioned in the directions might be helpful for the employee to use herself to implement these changes and become more productive?
3. Which of the ten strategies can Barbara's supervisor use to help this employee implement these changes and become more productive?

Facilitator Notes for Case Study 23

LEARNING OBJECTIVE: Given ten strategies and a case study, supervisors will apply specific strategies appropriately to the situation.

Possible Case Answers

1. Why is it difficult for employees to deal with these situations? Major changes are occurring rapidly. The changes come from changes in the law and employees at this level have no voice in how changes are implemented. Some employees do not respond well to technological changes.
2. Which of the ten strategies in the directions might be helpful for the employee to use herself to implement these changes and become more productive? Any or all of the strategies can be helpful. Get participants to explain their rationale and link suggestions to problems identified by the group.
3. Which of the ten strategies can Barbara's supervisor use to help this employee implement these changes and become more productive? Any or all of the strategies can be helpful. Get participants to explain their rationale and link suggestions to problems identified by the group.

Facilitator Processing Questions and Potential Answers

Q: Why is complex change difficult for employees?

A: Issues that are ignored seem to become bigger problems. Complex change situations involving large numbers of employees provide many opportunities for things to go wrong. The larger the organization, the more impersonal it seems, unless management works at personalizing the implementation and making employees a part of the process.

Q: Which of the five suggestions are appropriate to implement in your situation?

A: Answers will vary with the individual.

Change Management Serial Case Study

Several of the cases in this chapter can be combined as a progressive case study by changing the names of the individuals in the separate case studies to be the same person.

Facilitator Processing Questions and Potential Answers

Q: What are the most difficult situations for employees to deal with regarding organizational changes?

Q: What strategies are most effective in helping employees deal with resistance to change?

Q: What are strategies you can apply to implementing changes and reducing resistance for your employees?

A: Answers will vary according to the learners' situation.

7

Coaching and Mentoring

THIS CHAPTER contains five types of case studies that teach various lessons about how to coach and mentor subordinates. Case studies in this chapter might be used in "leadership" or "mentoring" workshops to help train those unfamiliar with how to be more effective in leading and developing others.

See the Introduction to Part 2 on pages 63–64 for suggestions on how to select and customize the case studies in this chapter.

COACHING AND MENTORING IDENTIFICATION CASE STUDY 24

You Don't Say!

Directions: What does an effective mentor or coach do to develop others? Read the following situation, then identify which of the mentor's questions or statements are appropriate. Also identify which questions might cause a defensive reaction from the person being coached or might not get her to reveal more about the actual situation. Use the "N" code if you are not sure what reaction the mentor or coach might evoke. For each set of statements or questions, label the options as:

A = appropriate

D = defensive

N = not sure of the other's reaction

Sandra is a volunteer mentor who has been working with Yolanda for about two months. Yolanda has been a resident of a homeless shelter for three months and has not been able to find employment. Yolanda is a recovering alcoholic and has been sober for the three months she has lived at the shelter. She regularly attends support meetings through a twelve-step program but resents the shelter requirements to have forty hours of productive time each week. Productive time is defined as time spent on education or training activities, looking for employment or volunteer activities at the shelter. Sandra is preparing for her next session with Yolanda.

1. Yolanda has been looking for a job for two months. Sandra wants to encourage Yolanda to continue her job search. Rate each statement using the A, D, N codes.
    a. "It's too bad you haven't found anything yet. What can I do to help you?"
    b. "What have you tried already and how has that worked?"

   c. "You'll never leave the shelter if you don't find a job. Why haven't you been able to find a job?"

2. Sandra has read Yolanda's resume and thinks that she has excellent work experience that could produce better results if the resume were rewritten. Rate each statement using the A, D, N codes.

   a. "Did you read the book on resume writing that I gave you last week?"

   b. "Your job experience needs to stand out more if you want to get an employer to notice it. Would you like me to rewrite it for you?"

   c. "Most employers review a resume to identify your job experience and skills. How can your resume be rewritten to make those two items more visible?"

3. Sandra is concerned that Yolanda is failing to make a positive impression on prospective employers because she has purple streaks in her black hair and has several visible body piercings. Rate each statement using the A, D, N codes.

   a. "What judgments do employers make about job candidates based on their physical appearance?"

   b. "Have you thought about removing your body piercings so they don't distract an employer during a job interview?"

   c. "You only have one chance to make a positive impression. Why do you think employers refuse to hire you?"

Facilitator Notes for Case Study 24

LEARNING OBJECTIVE: Given a case study, the coach or mentor will identify appropriate behavior that does not cause a defensive reaction to specific situations.

Possible Case Answers

Question code:

A = appropriate

D = defensive

N = not sure of the other's reaction

1. a = N. Yolanda might react well to this offer for help. However, mentors are usually in a position to know what they can do to help. "It's too bad" may cause a defensive reaction.
   b = A. This statement is appropriate since the mentor might not be aware of all of Yolanda's efforts and it's a good place to start a coaching conversation.
   c = D. This statement is likely to cause a defensive reaction and is punishing in tone.
2. a = N. While it is appropriate to find out if Yolanda has used a resource that Sandra provided, this is a "yes/no" question and will require some follow up to make the conversation more effective.
   b = D. While the statement is true, a mentor can be a better coach if she shows Yolanda how to rewrite the resume, rather than offer to do it for her.
   c = A. This question gets Yolanda to think for herself and is less judgmental.
3. a = A. This question is conversational and gets Yolanda to think of her own appearance without being judged.

b = N. This question is a "yes/no" question and could be interpreted by Yolanda as accusatory. Yolanda may have thought about the answer to this question herself. If Yolanda has a strong personality, she is likely to resent others for not getting to know her before judging her appearance.

c = D. The statement is given as a "fact." The question is also personalized so it becomes more difficult to discuss objectively.

Facilitator Processing Questions and Potential Answers

Q: What are characteristics of questions that cause a defensive reaction?

A: Characteristics of questions that easily cause a defensive reaction include accusatory, defensive, invasive, or personal questions.

Q: What are the characteristics of appropriate questions?

A: Characteristics of appropriate questions are helpful, factual, nonjudgmental, conversational, and encouraging.

Q: How would you word some of Sandra's appropriate questions to make them sound more like you speak?

A: The answers to this question would vary with each participant.

COACHING AND MENTORING PROBLEM SOLVING CASE STUDY 25

Get Back on Track

Directions: Read the following situation, then identify issues and problems. Write questions the mentor needs to ask the protégé to get their mentoring relationship back on track.

Sandra is a volunteer mentor who has been working with Yolanda for about two months. Yolanda has been a resident of a homeless shelter for three months and has not been able to find employment. Yolanda is a recovering alcoholic and has been sober for the three months she has lived at the shelter. She regularly attends support meetings through a twelve-step program but resents the shelter requirements to have forty hours of productive time each week. Productive time is defined as time spent on education or training activities, looking for employment, or volunteer activities at the shelter.

Yolanda cancelled her meeting with Sandra last week because she wasn't feeling well. Sandra is bright and energetic and very friendly. She also carefully plans all of her time so no opportunity is wasted. Sandra says, "Residents need structure if they are going to be successful." She put together a monthly plan for Yolanda that includes a different assignment each week to work on developing job-related skills and employment leads. Assignments include activities such as reading articles about job searching, resume writing, and calling employment agencies and large employers. Yolanda has done the minimal amount of work to complete some of the assignments.

Sandra isn't sure if she is helping Yolanda. She needs to find out why her mentoring efforts are not as productive as they have been with other protégés.

Identify issues and problems here.

What questions does the mentor need to ask the protégé?

Facilitator Notes for Case Study 25

LEARNING OBJECTIVE: Given a case study, identify the issues and problems in the situation and write questions for the mentor to ask to get the relationship back on track.

Possible Case Answers

The mentor in this case has been overly directive and can be more successful by helping the protégé learn planning skills, rather than impose them. Here are some questions to get the coaching and mentoring relationship back on track:

1. What is your objective for your job search?
2. What type of planning have you used before that will help you map out your search?
3. What job search hints did you find in the articles I left for you at our last meeting?
4. What barriers are you encountering in your search?
5. What can you do to overcome these barriers?
6. How can I best help you in your job search?

Facilitator Processing Questions and Potential Answers

Q: What do you notice about the questions that can get the mentoring relationship back on track?

A: Most questions treat the protégé as a peer. The questions are structured, yet make the protégé think for herself.

Q: What are the characteristics of less directive questions?

A: Most questions are open-ended and require some thought. The questions are supporting and helpful.

Q: How appropriate are less directive questions in your mentoring relationship?

A: Answers to this question will vary with each individual.

Q: How will you reword these questions to sound more like the way you talk?

A: Answers to this question will vary with each individual.

COACHING AND MENTORING PRACTICE CASE STUDY 26

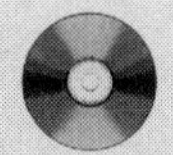

Coaching in a Mentoring Relationship

Directions: Read the following six levels of coaching, then read each situation and identify what level of coaching is appropriate and explain your answer. A mentor can be more effective if the appropriate level of coaching is provided. A good mentor can identify what level of coaching is appropriate based on what level of skill the other person possesses. The following is a list of six levels of coaching with each level showing an increased level of support and direction.

---

1. Identify: Point out or name deficiencies that the other person may not recognize. Example: *"There's a mistake on this report."*
2. Suggest: Offer advice or a suggestion. Example: *"This report would be easier to read if you move these key points to the beginning of the report."*
3. Explore: Help the other person develop or consider options. Example: *"What could help you identify mistakes more easily?"*
4. Guide: Help the other person implement a suggestion. Example: *"Let me walk you through some of these suggestions."*
5. Demonstrate: Show the other person how to do something correctly. Example: *"Let me show you how to eliminate this type of mistake."*
6. Instruct: Provide training in the absence of skill. Example: *"Here is how to avoid this type of mistake. I'll have you practice this process once you can answer some of my questions."*

If the other person being coached has some skill in the situation, then one of the first four levels of coaching are appropriate. If the other person has no skill, a demonstration or instruction will more quickly produce the desired result.

Situation 1: Brush-Up Training

A skilled new employee has just completed additional training to brush up on some interviewing techniques. In discussing how to interview for a specific job, she has made the same mistake twice.

What level would you suggest?

What is your rationale for this level?

What would you say?

Situation 2: Abrupt and Unfriendly Clerk

The new employee you are mentoring is on the telephone making an appointment for a job interview. Her questions to the store manager are great. However, she is very abrupt and unfriendly in dealing with the clerk who schedules the appointments.

What level would you suggest?

What is your rationale for this level?

What would you say?

Situation 3: Repeats the Same Mistake

A new employee has repeated the same mistake she made when practicing for an interview. She has not responded well to verbal directions.

What level would you suggest?

What is your rationale for this level?

What would you say?

Facilitator Notes for Case Study 26

LEARNING OBJECTIVE: Given a case study and a six-level model of coaching and mentoring, the coach or mentor will use one or more of the six levels for each case study situation.

Possible Case Answers

Situation 1: Brush-Up Training

Suggested level is "explore" or "guide." The rationale for this level is that the employee is new and might not be aware of two prior mistakes. If she doesn't know what else to do to avoid these mistakes, the mentor can move to the "demonstrate" or "instruct" level. You could say, "You don't seem to be getting the best reaction from that statement. What else can you say to get a better reaction?"

Situation 2: Abrupt and Unfriendly Clerk

Suggested level is "identify" or "suggest." The rationale for this level is this person might not be aware of her abrupt behavior toward the clerk. Being nice to a person scheduling an appointment is more about attitude than skill. You could say, "Why do you think the clerk scheduling the appointment was reserved and kept you on hold for 10 minutes to book a simple appointment?"

Situation 3: Repeats the Same Mistake

The suggested level is "demonstrate," since the employee is not responding to verbal directions, she might need to see and try out the technique before learning it. You could say, "Let me show you what I mean. I'll pretend to be you and you play the manager. Ask me the next question and see what you think of my answer."

Facilitator Processing Questions and Potential Answers

Q: What factors help you decide which level of coaching is appropriate in a given situation?

A: If the person being coached has some skill in the situation, then one of the first four levels of coaching is appropriate. If the person has no skill, a demonstration or instruction will more quickly produce the desired result. If the coach is not sure of the skill level, start with the "explore" level and ask a few questions. Then proceed to a higher or lower level, based on the skills of the person being coached.

Q: What could be the consequence of using too high a level of coaching, especially for a mature and skilled employee?

A: Overcoaching a mature and skilled employee can cause resentment and defensiveness.

Q: What could be the consequence of using too low a coaching level, especially for a new and unskilled employee?

A: Undercoaching a new or unskilled employee causes confusion, since that person does not have the skill to remedy the situation.

Q: How will you alter your coaching style with your subordinates?

A: This answer will vary for each coach.

COACHING AND MENTORING APPLICATION CASE STUDY 27

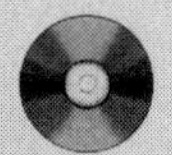

Coaching Isn't Doing

Directions: Read the coaching and mentoring techniques that follow. Mentors and coaches can develop protégés by providing the right information at the right time. Next, read the case study, then identify how to apply these coaching and mentoring techniques.

- **Be a question coach.** Mentors do not have all the answers, but they can help their protégés self-discover. Use questions to reflect on their experiences and draw out key learning points . . .
  - "What did you learn from this situation?"
  - "How might you approach this situation in the future?"
  - "What patterns are you noticing about yourself?"
- **Shine a new light.** Mentors have distance from their protégé's work problems and trials. Use this distance to . . .
  - Provide the "big picture" as a context for daily ups and downs
  - Take a long view, and teach your protégé to do the same
- **Let actions speak louder than words.** Most people learn by doing, so bring your protégé along when you can . . .
  - Ask your protégé to join you on projects that will expand his or her point of view.
  - Look at your own job for situations that could provide learning experiences.
  - Spend time debriefing the events and relating them to the new employee's development.
  - Ask for feedback from your protégé—you may learn something invaluable!

Sandra is a volunteer mentor who has been working with Yolanda for about two months. Yolanda has been a resident of a homeless shelter for three months and has not been able to find employment. Yolanda is a recovering alcoholic and has been sober for the three months she has lived at the shelter. She regularly attends support meetings through a twelve-step program but resents the shelter requirements to have forty hours of productive time each week. Productive time is defined as time spent on education or training activities, looking for employment, or volunteer activities at the shelter.

In the two months Sandra has mentored and coached Yolanda, her approach has been very directive and "hands on." Yolanda's work experience has been in the medical records field. With the shortages in qualified people for this type of work, Sandra is surprised Yolanda's job search hasn't been more successful. How can Sandra apply the coaching and mentoring skills and "be a question coach" or "shine a new light" or "let actions speak louder than words"?

Facilitator Notes for Application Case Study 27

LEARNING OBJECTIVE: Given a case study, apply three non-directive coaching and mentoring techniques appropriately in each situation.

Possible Case Answers

Sandra can be an effective "question coach" if she asks Yolanda open-ended questions that begin with "what" and "how." Her overly directive style seems to be making Yolanda defensive, and Yolanda could learn more by doing her own planning activities.

"Shining a new light" could help Yolanda see work in a new perspective. Helping Yolanda focus on some time in her life when she was successful could be helpful. Helping Yolanda develop longer-term goals than finding a job will allow Yolanda to make her own plans to get there.

"Actions" can definitely help Yolanda and give her more to think about. Informational interviewing with employed people in the medical records field might be helpful. Discussing what others like about their jobs can be a good learning experience for this protégé.

Facilitator Processing Questions and Potential Answers

Q: What is the consequence for the protégé of having a mentor or coach do too much for them rather than teaching the protégé new skills?

A: The consequences could be that the protégé will not learn any new skills and become more dependent on the mentor.

Q: What are appropriate options for a coach or mentor who does too much for the protégé?

A: Mentors are more effective if they provide new information, show the protégé a new perspective, and open doors that have been closed to the protégé. An effective mentor supports the actions of the protégé, rather than taking direct action. Use techniques to build confidence, discuss past successes, and provide encouragement.

Coaching and Mentoring Serial Case Study

All of the case studies in this chapter are about the same mentor. Taken together, they form a progressive case study. The following Facilitator Processing Questions can tie all of the previous case studies together.

Coaching and Mentoring: Serial Case Study

LEARNING OBJECTIVE: Given a series of case studies, identify characteristics of effective coaches or mentors and overcome barriers to being a more effective coach or mentor.

Facilitator Processing Questions and Potential Answers

Q: What are the characteristics of effective coaches and mentors?

A: Effective coaches and mentors:

- Offer the right level of coaching, neither too little nor too much. Start with "exploring" the situation by asking questions if not sure which is the right level.
- Make appropriate statements and ask appropriate questions that encourage and explore and do not make the protégé defensive or embarrassed.
- Ask questions and use a non-directive approach.
- Give the protégé a new perspective that is difficult to see from the current situation.
- Helps place the protégé in new situations with the right amount of support and motivation.

Q: What is the difference between a coach and a mentor?

A: A coach can be a peer as well as someone in a more responsible position in the hierarchy. A coach is someone who has skills the protégé needs to acquire. A mentor is usually more than one step above the protégé in a hierarchy. A mentor is most valuable when a different point of view is available and provides access to new opportunities by opening doors that were previously closed.

Q: What pitfalls create barriers for being an effective coach or mentor?

A: As seen from the previous cases, over-directing and doing too much for the protégé that the protégé ought to do for himself or herself is counterproductive. Not selecting the appropriate level of coaching (from the six levels offered earlier in the skill practice case study) can cause resentment or confusion.

Q: How can a coach or mentor overcome pitfalls and remove barriers?

A: Be clear about your relationship with the protégé. Ask more questions and find out what the protégé wants out of the relationship.

Q: What can you do to be a more effective coach or mentor?

A: This answer will vary with each participant.

8

Customer Service

THIS CHAPTER contains five types of case studies that teach various lessons about customer service. Case studies in this chapter might be used to teach skills for those who work in a call center on the telephone or deal with customers face-to-face. The case studies might also be useful in "quality improvement" or "customer service management" workshops to help train those unfamiliar with how to be more effective in dealing with customers.

See the Introduction to Part 2 on pages 63–64 for suggestions on how to select and customize the case studies in this chapter.

CUSTOMER SERVICE IDENTIFICATION CASE STUDY 28

Personal Job Responsibilities

Directions: In each of these situations, identify what the employee needs to do to more effectively accomplish his or her responsibilities as an empowered employee.

1. A landscape architect is designing a garden for a young family of four people: two adults and two children (ages 8 and 10). This couple is excited about owning a new house. Previously they had lived in an apartment. The trees, shrubs, and flowers that could be planted are numerous. The family is looking forward to entertaining family and friends in their new garden.

   What does the landscape architect need to do?

2. You have just made airline and hotel reservations to go to a city where you have not been before. You ask the travel agent about ground transportation to reach your hotel and she replies, "Well I can get you a rental car, or just look around when you come out of the baggage claim area. There's usually lots of taxis, buses, or cars for hire."

   What does the travel agent need to do?

3. After purchasing a new suit from a department store, you find a flaw in the fabric and return it to the store. The only replacement suit at this location is a size larger. The clerk offers to give you back your money.

   What does the salesclerk need to do?

Facilitator Notes for Case Study 28

LEARNING OBJECTIVE: Given a case study, employees will identify appropriate behavior for empowered behaviors.

Possible Case Answers

Empowered employees would be able to make decisions and take actions without approval from a supervisor. Here are suggestions for what empowered employees can do in these three case studies:

1. The landscape architect needs to ask the family questions about how they plan to use the new garden. Also, he or she needs to ask about the types of trees, shrubs, and flowers that they would like in their garden. The landscape architect also needs to offer the family choices.
2. The travel agent can offer to investigate the distance from the airport to the hotel, the variety and cost of different modes of ground transportation, and offer to make a reservation for the type of transportation the customer prefers.
3. The department store clerk can offer to find the correct size at another location and have it sent to the customer, offer the same suit in another color, or offer to have the fabric flaw repaired, if possible.

Facilitator Processing Questions and Potential Answers

Q: Based on the three case studies, what do you expect empowered employees to do to act responsibly?

A: An empowered employee asks the customer questions, offers options, and tries to make the situation better.

Q: What are the characteristics of an empowered employee?

A: Characteristics of an empowered employee include initiative, empathy, decisive, caring, trustworthy, humble, and capable.

Q: What prevents you from being an empowered employee?

A: Although answers may vary with individuals, typical answers may include lack of authority, close supervision, lack of options, or not caring.

Q: What can you do to overcome the barriers to being an empowered employee?

A: To overcome these barriers, the empowered employee needs to work in cooperation with a supervisor, have an incentive to be empowered, and the capacity to develop the characteristics of an empowered employee.

CUSTOMER SERVICE PROBLEM SOLVING CASE STUDY 29

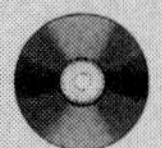

Hurry Up!

Directions: Write questions to help the customer service representative (CSR) identify the problem accurately and develop options to offer this customer.

Brenda is a CSR at an Appliance Repair and Service Call Center. Her primary job is to answer questions about the types of appliances her company repairs, the cost of a service call, when service might be available, and troubleshoot repairs in progress. She gets a call from an owner of a laundromat who is a good and recurring customer. The company's technician, who is onsite now at the laundromat, is a new field repair technician. The owner is upset with the length of time the repairs are taking and the fact that the technician says two machines are beyond repair.

1. What questions will you ask this laundromat owner to identify the problem correctly?
2. What options will you offer this customer?

Facilitator Notes for Case Study 29

LEARNING OBJECTIVE: Given a case study, ask accurate questions to uncover the problem correctly and develop at least two options to offer this customer.

Possible Case Answers

1. Questions to ask this customer to uncover the problem might include:
   - What is the make and model of each machine requiring repair?
   - What type of service is the owner requesting for each machine?
   - What is the problem that the field technician has identified?
   - How long has the technician been working on the repair?
   - What reason(s) did the technician give for the two machines being beyond repair?
2. Options you could offer this customer might include:
   - You will talk directly with the technician to find out why the repairs are taking so long.
   - You will have the technician's supervisor call the owner and/or the technician within the next half hour.
   - Make an adjustment on the charges if the technician should have found the source of the problem sooner.
   - Ask the owner what type of remedy he wants.

Facilitator Processing Questions and Potential Answers

Q: What types of questions help identify the problem correctly?

A: A combination of open-ended and closed-ended questions helps get enough information to identify the problem correctly.

Q: How much information do you need to develop before offering a customer options or making a decision about how to resolve the problem?

A: Once the customer has agreed with how you have identified the problem, you can proceed with options for resolution.

Q: What are characteristics of appropriately worded problem-solving questions?

A: Problem-solving questions are worded so the person answering the question does not get defensive, are open-ended to gain information, and are closed-ended when asking for clarification or agreement.

Q: What are characteristics of appropriate options?

A: Appropriate options are reasonable in time, cost, and value for you and the customer and can be delivered realistically and efficiently. The customer must be agreeable to the option for the solution to work.

Q: What problem-solving skills do you need to develop and how will you do that?

A: This answer will vary with the individual.

CUSTOMER SERVICE PRACTICE CASE STUDY 30

What's the Question?

Directions: Read the case study, then write appropriate open-ended questions to let the customer tell his story without interruption and appropriately closed-ended questions to control the conversation, clarify the customer's point, gain agreement, or summarize the call.

Brenda is a Customer Service Representative (CSR) at an Appliance Repair and Service Call Center. Her primary job is to answer questions about the types of appliances her company repairs, the cost of a service call, when service might be available, and troubleshoot repairs in progress. She gets a call from an owner of a laundromat who is a "good" and recurring customer. The company's technician, who is onsite now at the laundromat, is a new field repair technician. The owner is upset with the length of time the repairs are taking and the fact that the technician says two machines are beyond repair.

- What are appropriate open-ended questions to get the customer's story?
- What are appropriate closed-ended questions to control the conversation, clarify the customer's point of view, gain agreement, or summarize the call?

Facilitator Notes for Case Study 30

LEARNING OBJECTIVE: Given a case study, the CSR will ask appropriately worded open-ended and closed-ended questions to control the conversation, clarify the customer's point, gain agreement, or summarize the call.

Possible Case Answers

1. Appropriately worded open-ended questions include:
   - What is the problem that the field technician has identified?
   - What reason(s) did the technician give for the two machines being beyond repair?
   - What do you think is wrong with the machine?
2. Appropriately worded closed-ended questions include:
   - Control the call:
     - What is the make and model of each machine requiring repair?
     - What type of service is the owner requesting for each machine?
     - How long has the technician been working on the repair?
   - Clarify the customer's point of view:
     - The reason you're unhappy with the service call so far is that it's taking too much time? Is that right?
   - Gain agreement:
     - Do you agree with the problem the technician has identified?
   - Summarize the call:
     - Can I have our supervising technician call you back within 30 minutes?

Facilitator Processing Questions and Potential Answers

Q: What are characteristics of appropriately worded open-ended questions?

A: Appropriately worded open-ended questions:

Begin with *what, how,* and *why*

Can be prepared in advance in a job aid

Can be asking for fact and/or opinion

Require time for the other person to think before answering

Don't make the other person defensive (so avoid asking lots of "why" questions)

Q: What are characteristics of appropriately worded closed-ended questions?

A: Appropriately worded closed-end questions:

Begin with *are, can, did, do, which, when*

Can ask for identifying information

Can ask the other person to make a limited choice

Are worded to control the conversation

Q: What types of questions do you need to word better in your situation?

A: Answers to this question will vary with the participant.

CUSTOMER SERVICE APPLICATION CASE STUDY 31

Principles of Customer Service

Directions: Table 8.1 lists the four principles of customer service and examples of how to apply each principle with customers. Read the case study that follows, and identify how well the four principles are applied. How did the hotel employees in the case apply these principles? What can be done better?

Table 8.1. Four Principles of Customer Service.

Principle:	*What It Means:*
Trustworthy	• Make sure customers get what they want. • Keep your word; be reliable and dependable.
Caring	• Talk the customer's language. • Listen for facts and feelings. • Show respect; convey trust and confidence. • Express empathy, not sympathy. • Show interest in the other person's needs. • Be responsive to the customer's needs.
Humble	• Use an appropriate tone of voice. • Be courteous. Say "please" and "thank you."
Capable	• Provide prompt service; tell people how you can assist them. • Be knowledgeable. • Use or provide facilities and equipment well. • Be prepared. • Avoid errors.

Sally was weary by the time she arrived at her hotel. Her plane was delayed by bad weather, the line at the rental car agency was very long, and the highway to the hotel was congested with rush-hour traffic. All she wanted to do was eat a late dinner and get some sleep before the important sales meeting the next morning.

After arriving at her room, Sally noticed the room was extremely warm. She turned on the air conditioner and when no improvement occurred, she phoned the front desk to ask for someone to check the unit in her room. The front desk clerk said, "Oh, honey, don't worry about the room temperature. It just takes a while to cool the rooms during extremely warm days." Sally went to the lobby restaurant to find it was closed. She asked the bellman about dinner options and he directed her to vending machines off the lobby, or she could order a pizza delivered to her room by a local take-out restaurant. He gave her a coupon for $1 off a large pizza and said, "I work at this place on the weekends and it's really good."

Sally decided to ask the bell captain for other options besides stale crackers, candy, and pizza. The bell captain said most area restaurants were already closed, but room service is available for another hour. That might be her best option. Sally told the bell captain about the room temperature problem in her room. He said he would be pleased to order her meal from his telephone and told her it could be served in the hotel lounge. He also offered to call the hotel engineer and have the air conditioner in her room checked.

When Sally was finishing her dinner in the hotel lounge, the bell captain informed her that the air conditioning unit was old and needed to be replaced. Since it was getting late, he suggested Sally move to another room. He offered to get her new room key and assist her in moving to another room.

How did the hotel employees in this case apply the four principles of customer service?

What can be done better?

Facilitator Notes for Case Study 31

LEARNING OBJECTIVE: Given a case study, the CSR will identify how well four customer service principles are applied, and identify what employees can do differently to apply all four principles.

Possible Case Answers

1. How did the hotel employees in this case apply the four principles of customer service?
   - Trustworthy: The bell captain made sure the hotel guest, Sally, got dinner and an air-conditioned room.
   - Caring: The bell captain showed an interest in the guest's needs.
   - Humble: The bell captain said he would be pleased to order her meal.
   - Capable: The bell captain told Sally how he could assist getting her to another room.
2. What can be done better?
   - Trustworthy: The front desk clerk and bellman did not get Sally what she wanted.
   - Caring: The front desk clerk didn't seem to care about the room temperature. The bellman seemed to think crackers and candy from a vending machine or delivered pizza was an appropriate option.
   - Humble: The front desk clerk inappropriately addressed the guest as "honey."
   - Capable: The front desk clerk was not prepared to assist the guest with timely options that would appeal to this guest and meet her needs.

Facilitator Processing Questions and Potential Answers

Q: What makes it easy or difficult for hotel employees to provide appropriate customer service that is based on the four principles?

A: An employee's attitude can make it easy or difficult to act on the four principles. How management reinforces or rewards the application of the principles has to play a role.

Q: What are additional principles of customer service that are appropriate for how you help our customers? Give an example that demonstrates the importance of this principle.

A: Answers and examples will vary with individuals.

Q: What will you do to apply the four customer service principles?

A: Answers and examples will vary with individuals.

CUSTOMER SERVICE SERIAL CASE STUDY 32

Customer Service Standards

Directions: Use the four previous case studies in this chapter, then identify the principles of customer service that are appropriate for your organization. Express the principles in terms of standards that meet the customer's expectations (See Table 8.2.)

POSSIBLE CASE ANSWERS

Table 8.2. Suggested Customer Service Standards.

Principle:	*What It Means:*	*Example of a Standard:*
Trustworthy	• Make sure customers get what they want. • Keep your word; be reliable and dependable.	• Satisfaction guaranteed or your money back. • Packages delivered overnight or your money back.
Caring	• Talk the customer's language. • Listen for facts and feelings. • Show respect; convey trust and confidence. • Express empathy, not sympathy. • Show interest in the other person's needs. • Be responsive to the customer's needs.	• The airline will provide a discount meal coupon if your flight is delayed by more than two hours.

(Continued)

Table 8.2. Suggested Customer Service Standards (Continued).

Principle:	*What It Means:*	*Example of a Standard:*
Humble	• Use an appropriate tone of voice. • Be courteous. Say "please" and "thank you."	• Address the customer by name. • Thank a customer for an opportunity to provide service or service recovery.
Capable	• Provide prompt service; tell people how you can assist them. • Be knowledgeable. • Use or provide facilities and equipment well. • Be prepared. • Avoid errors.	• Your luggage will be delivered to your room in 15 minutes from check-in or less. • A customer will be called back with progress toward the resolution of their complaint within 30 minutes. • The server will check back with the restaurant patron 5 minutes after the meal is served.

Facilitator Processing Questions and Potential Answers

Q: How easy or difficult is it to create standards of service written from the customer's point of view?

Q: What are possible barriers for employees to meet these standards?

Q: How can these barriers be overcome?

Q: How will we measure these standards?

Q: How often will we measure these standards?

Q: What can you do to meet these standards?

A: All answers will vary with each employee and organization.

9

Diversity

THIS CHAPTER contains five types of case studies that teach various lessons about diversity. Case studies in this chapter might be used to teach skills for those who work in teams or supervise a diverse work group. The case studies might also be useful in "supervision" or "intercultural sensitivity" workshops to help train those unfamiliar with how to be more effective in dealing with diverse work groups.

See the Introduction to Part 2 on pages 63–64 for suggestions on how to select and customize the case studies in this chapter.

DIVERSITY IDENTIFICATION CASE STUDY 33

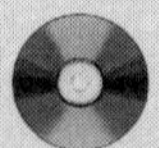

What Do You See?

Directions: In their book, Managing Diversity *(McGraw-Hill, 1998), Lee Gardenschwartz and Anita Rowe identify six internal dimensions of diversity: age, gender, sexual orientation, physical ability, ethnicity, and race. As you read the case study, identify the bias around the six dimensions for the team leader and team members.*

Bill supervises a work group of twelve people at a Northern California high-tech manufacturing plant in the packaging and shipping department. Bill is a white male who is looking forward to his retirement in three years. Previously, Bill had heard rumors of some crude jokes told by some men on the team and now Rosie, the senior woman in the group, reported a complaint at the end of yesterday's shift. Bill said he would investigate and told her not to take a comment from a "good ole boy" personally.

Bill's team is made up of three white men (Randy, Bob, and Steve) in their mid-50s who have worked together the longest of all the employees. Said and Mohammed are Arab-American immigrants from Egypt who are in their mid-30s. Randy, Bob, and Steve often complain to Bill about Said and Mohammed because they speak in Arabic and are probably talking about them. Rosie, Yolanda, Maria, and Loretta are second-generation immigrants from the Mexican State of Sonora in their mid-30s. They are cousins or best friends from high school and have been accused by some men in their group of gossiping, always talking about their kids, cooking, and social events, which is distracting for those on the team that are trying to work. Bill has noticed that Loretta is quite overweight and the other three women often do the more physically difficult parts of the job for her. The youngest team members are men in their late 20s. Nguyen, Tran, and Jimmy are second-generation immigrants from Vietnam whose parents arrived in California in the early 1980s as refugees. The three young men are not related and their families originated from different regions of Vietnam. All three regard themselves as completely

Americanized, having been born and attended 12 years of school in the United States. Their parents are proud that the young men are all attending community college in the evenings and studying computer science. Jimmy refused an assignment to work on a special project with another work group. Bill thought he just wasn't interested and lacks initiative, like a lot of young kids today. Bill commented, "I thought all you Asians were so ambitious."

When Bill discusses the crude remarks with Randy, Bob, and Steve, Bob complains back to Bill, "Those gossipy women have nothing better to do than listen in on our conversations. I was just telling the guys a joke before our team meeting started. Those women were coming in late again. Them and the Arabs sure have that 'mañana' attitude, always coming late to team meetings."

Identify the bias around the six dimensions for the team leader and team members. The six internal dimensions of diversity are age, gender, sexual orientation, physical ability, ethnicity, and race.

Facilitator Notes for Case Study 33

LEARNING OBJECTIVE: Given a case study, the team member will identify biases of individuals around the six dimensions of internal diversity: age, gender, sexual orientation, physical ability, ethnicity, and race.

Possible Case Answers

Age: Four white males are 20–30 years older than the other team members. Team leader, Bill, seems to think young people lack initiative.

Gender: Some men on the team accuse the four women of gossiping and talking about their families rather than paying attention to their work. What one woman considers a crude joke, the men think of as harmless.

Sexual orientation: No examples provided in this case study.

Physical ability: Bill thinks the other three women are doing part of Loretta's work because she is overweight.

Ethnicity: Bob thinks Arabs and Mexicans are tardy and perhaps lazy.

Race: Bill thinks all Asians are ambitious.

Facilitator Processing Questions and Potential Answers

Q: What makes it difficult for us to see our own biases?

A: We are often not aware of our own culture until taken out of it. If a person associates with and befriends only people like himself or herself, then differences are beyond that person's awareness.

Q: How are biases formed and perpetuated?

A: We are all "captives of our culture" according to Edward Hall, an anthropologist. Biases are formed as a part of growing up. We absorb the values of our family and friends as normal. What is different is often seen and interpreted as not normal. We judge the behavior of others based on our norms. So, if someone is different, that is often interpreted as inferior, bad, or reason for suspicion. For example, in American culture, eye contact between a parent (authority figure) and a child assures communication and that the child is listening to the parent. In Hispanic cultures eye contact with an authority figure is a sign of defiance and disrespect. So if a Hispanic does not make eye contact with a White authority figure, that behavior could be interpreted as an unwillingness to take correction. The White authority figure could conclude that the Hispanic will continue with that behavior, only be more covert about it. It becomes easy for the person outside another's culture to judge all people in that culture the same way. In that way, a behavior becomes a stereotype.

Q: What can be done to overcome bias?

A: Awareness and education about differences that are just as valid as one's own is a critical part of overcoming bias. The more contact people have outside their own culture, the more they see that stereotypes are not valid and that differences are neither good nor bad. They are just different.

Q: What biases do you have and how can you become more aware of them and overcome them?

A: Answers will vary with individuals.

DIVERSITY PROBLEM SOLVING CASE STUDY 34

What's the Problem?

Directions: State the problem you are trying to resolve. Identify what questions you think the team leader should ask of the employee making the complaint and of the employee who made the crude jokes.

Bill supervises a work group of twelve people at a Northern California high-tech manufacturing plant in the packaging and shipping department. Bill is a white male who is looking forward to his retirement in three years. Previously, Bill had heard rumors of some crude jokes told by some men on the team and now Rosie, the senior woman in the group, reported a complaint at the end of yesterday's shift.

- State the problem you are trying to resolve.
- Identify what questions you think the team leader should ask of the employee making the complaint and of the employee who made the crude jokes.

Facilitator Notes for Case Study 34

LEARNING OBJECTIVE: Given a case study, state the problem and identify appropriate questions to ask of the two employees involved in the problem case study.

Possible Case Answers

State the problem you are trying to resolve: Disharmony in the work team due to lack of understanding about how one person's remarks are interpreted by another employee.

Questions for the team leader of the employee making the complaint:

- What did you hear the other employee say?
- What made his remarks offensive to you?
- Were these remarks made directly to you or was it something you overheard?
- Has this person made similar remarks directly to you before? If so, what was said and when?
- What do you expect me to do about these remarks that would restore team harmony?

Questions for the team leader of the employee who made the crude jokes:

- What was said by you that could be characterized as a crude joke that was heard by the other employee?
- What did you say that could be considered as offensive by another team member? What is the basis for the other employee finding these remarks offensive?
- What can you do to demonstrate respect for other team members?

Facilitator Processing Questions and Potential Answers

Q: How is it that remarks by one employee appear humorous to some and as offensive to others?

A: When a team has internally diverse members, insensitivity to others can easily cause offense.

Q: What elements of team harmony can be disrupted by insensitivity to someone else's internal diversity (age, gender, sexual orientation, physical ability, ethnicity, and race)?

A: Insensitivity to internal diversity issues causes team members to assume that others are just like them. If he is not offended, then no one else is offended. If others are different, then the other's situation is judged to be less. When team members see others as unequal, that translates into lack of trust, jealousy, annoyance that others are not contributing equally to the team and so on.

Q: How can team harmony be restored?

A: Team harmony can be established or restored when all team members see each other as equals, regardless of differences in the six internal diversity areas. Awareness, training, and experiences about diversity can help bring about sensitivity to others. New information and experiences can help make an irritation over a difference understandable. Unless team members get to the point of "different is OK" there will not be team harmony.

Q: What causes disharmony in your work team? Are any of these issues related to internal diversity issues?

A: Issues related to disharmony and internal diversity will vary with each team.

Q: What can be done to restore or establish harmony related to internal diversity?

A: Certainly acknowledging differences and finding common groups is an important step in building team harmony. Talking with all team members individually and as a group to clarify expectations, honor preferences, and providing feedback and coaching will help to build team harmony.

DIVERSITY PRACTICE CASE STUDY 35

Let Me Tell You

Directions: Bill, the White team leader who is a few years away from retirement, is giving feedback and coaching Rosie, a second-generation Hispanic woman in her mid-30s. To give feedback skillfully, Bill needs to provide feedback that is free of cultural bias.

Appropriate intercultural feedback has five characteristics:

1. **Describe** what needs to be done using an "I" message, rather than making a judgment.

   EXAMPLE: **"I need to discuss this idea with others in the department before deciding what to do."**

   NOT: "This idea is awful."

2. Stick to the **here and now.** Avoid the use of the words **always** and **never.**

   EXAMPLE: **"Trying this idea has certain risks for the customer. Let's evaluate them."**

   NOT: "This will never work. We've always done it this way."

3. Promote the employee's **self-esteem.**

   EXAMPLE: **"It would help me evaluate your questions if I knew more details about why this procedure causes a problem."**

   NOT: "You've got to be kidding about this suggestion."

4. Focus on a **specific behavior,** which the employee can do something about. Avoid comparisons.

   EXAMPLE: **"Your suggestions can be evaluated more quickly if reasons are given to support a suggestion."**

   NOT: "Randy's suggestions are so much more complete than yours."

5. Give **specific information** and a "real" answer.

   EXAMPLE: **"If we stop using form XYZ, we will not have the information needed to process the order."**

   NOT: "We can't do that. Manufacturing won't let us."

As you read the case, assess how well Bill is using appropriate intercultural feedback.

Bill has noticed that Rosie has been doing part of Loretta's job. Loretta is overweight and finds it difficult to perform some of the more physically demanding parts of her job in the packaging and shipping department. He wants to be sure all employees have equitable work as a part of the team. These are statements that Bill has made to Rosie as part of his feedback and coaching discussion.

1. "Rosie, you've been helping the other girls out by doing their work."
2. "I'm concerned that everyone has an equitable workload."
3. "When Loretta needs to file shipping documents in hard-to-reach places, what options are available for her to do the filing herself?"
4. "You always seem to rescue Loretta, instead of letting her find ways to do her job."
5. "Some of your work is suffering because you take on the work of others."

Facilitator Notes for Case Study 35

LEARNING OBJECTIVE: Given a case study involving feedback statements from the team leader, identify statements that use the principles of appropriate intercultural feedback. If the principles are not used appropriately, reword the team leader's statement.

Possible Case Answers

1. "Rosie, you've been helping the other girls out by doing their work."
   This statement does not use an "I" message. It is neither descriptive nor specific. The term *girls* is inappropriate. Use *women* instead.
   Reworded statement: "Rosie, I noticed you have assisted Loretta by filing documents in hard-to-reach places."
2. "I'm concerned that everyone has an equitable workload."
   This statement is not specific. "Equitable workload" needs to be explained.
   Reworded statement: "I'm concerned that when you volunteer to do some of Loretta's work, that you are doing more than you are required to do. Is Loretta offering to do some of your work in return?"
3. "When Loretta needs to file shipping documents in hard-to-reach places, what options are available for her to do the filing herself?"
   This appropriately worded statement is specific and asks a question that encourages discussion.
4. "You always seem to rescue Loretta, instead of letting her find ways to do her job."
   This statement is not specific, exaggerated, and the term *rescue* probably overstates the case.
   Reworded statement: "By helping Loretta when a task is physically challenging, you may be encouraging her to depend too heavily on

you to do an essential part of her job. How could you encourage Loretta to become more independent?"

5. "Some of your work is suffering because you take on the work of others."
   This statement is not specific; it is judgmental and accusatory.
   Reworded statement: "I'm concerned that you are not finishing your work by the end of each day and spending time helping Loretta file shipping documents that are a part of her job."

Facilitator Processing Questions and Potential Answers

Q: What makes it easy or difficult to use appropriately worded intercultural feedback?

A: Individual answers may vary according to the participants. Certainly an awareness of the other person's cultural norms would be helpful.

Q: Besides the five we have provided, what are other characteristics of appropriately worded intercultural feedback?

A: Other characteristics might include avoiding evaluating another's behavior and stating feedback in a positive manner, rather than in the negative form. Focus on what the other person can do, rather than what they need to stop doing. Also consider how feedback is delivered to a person from another culture. Some cultures value indirectness, and being extremely direct may prove embarrassing and cause an unintentional loss of face.

Q: How will you modify your feedback in intercultural conversations?

A: The answers to this question will vary with individuals.

DIVERSITY APPLICATION CASE STUDY 36

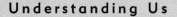

Understanding Us

Directions: In their book, Managing Diversity *(McGraw Hill, 1999), Lee Gardenschwartz and Anita Rowe identify five "American Cultural Norms" that can be shared with individuals raised in a culture outside the United States. In this case study, the team leader attempts helping employees from other cultures understand their American counterparts more easily and apply different behaviors in culturally appropriate ways. The five "American Cultural Norms" are*

- *Emphasis on promptness and time*
- *Direct explicit communication*
- *Competitive spirit*
- *Rugged individualism*
- *Informality in relationships*

As you read the case study, identify how well the team leader, Bill, applies this explanation to his multicultural team. What else could Bill have said or done to help others understand their American co-workers?

Bill explains the following to his team, "Our company places great emphasis on getting to work and meetings on time. When we say the meeting will start at 10:00 AM, we mean it will start exactly at 10:00 AM; not 10:07 AM or 10:15 AM. If it is important enough for us to meet together to discuss an issue, then it is important not to waste one another's time by showing up late. In our culture, showing up late and unprepared for a meeting is a sign of disrespect for others."

"Some of you have also been casual about how much time you take for a break. Breaks are 15 minutes, so please keep breaks to that amount of time."

"Americans can sometimes be blunt and direct in how we speak to each other. We think it is important to speak directly and avoid misunderstanding. Please realize that we are not insulting you when we speak so directly. Loretta, I overheard Randy ask you for some shipping documents. I could tell by the look on your face that you might have been offended by how he asked for them. He was in a hurry and didn't intend to insult you."

"We also tend to be informal and call each other by our first names, regardless of how old another person may be. That is not seen by us as disrespectful, rather it is our way of showing that we are all equal."

Facilitator Notes for Case Study 36

LEARNING OBJECTIVE: Given a case study, identify how well the team leader explains American culture to his diverse team.

Possible Case Answers

How well does the team leader, Bill, apply his explanation to his multicultural team?

- Bill explains that promptness is a company norm, not just an American expectation.
- Bill does well in explaining the concepts of directness and informality.

What else could Bill have said or done to help others understand their American co-workers?

- Bill's third statement is about American directness. It might help his team understand the entire message if he began with that point, rather than opening his comments with punctuality.
- Bill missed an opportunity to talk about individualism and competitiveness and how those two ideas might run counter to an effective team. If he is going to build a cohesive team, he needs to discuss how all team members view these concepts and how those views affect the team's success.
- Although Bill explains the concepts of directness and informality appropriately, he gives an example to the team that might have embarrassed the two team members involved. Bill does not address how directness and informality affects the team or how all team members can or should behave.

Facilitator Processing Questions and Potential Answers

Q: What makes it easy or difficult to explain the five American Cultural Norms to those not raised in American culture?

A: Unless you are aware of cultural norms and differences, you might not have thought about how Americans appear to those outside this culture. Unless you have experienced other cultures, it is easy to assume that everyone has norms similar to your own.

Q: Do you agree with the five American Cultural Norms? What would you add or delete from this list as norms?

A: Answers will be different for each participant. Ask participants to provide a rationale or example for other norms they might suggest.

Q: How would you explain these norms to someone outside American culture?

A: Answers will be different for each participant and the situation. Help participants understand that explanations are received well when they are not made in a comparative manner that implies that one norm is better than another. They are just different.

Diversity Serial Case Study

The four preceding case studies are about the same team and can be combined to address a variety of diversity issues when used in the same workshop. The four cases begin with identifying inappropriate behavior for a diverse team. Problems caused by insensitive behavior are identified along with suggestions. The third case develops diversity sensitive feedback, and the fourth case helps team members understand the norms of another group. After discussing all four case studies, ask the additional facilitator processing questions below.

Facilitator Processing Questions and Potential Answers

Q: The previous case study raised issues around internal diversity dimensions. Gardenschwartz and Rowe also identify external diversity dimensions, such as educational background, marital status, religion, and income. Further, they identify organizational dimensions such as seniority, functional level, work location, union affiliation, and so on. Do any of these other diversity dimensions present issues in your organization?

Q: What have you learned about understanding those who are different as well as assumptions you make about those differences?

Q: How will you behave differently to honor differences?

Q: What other experiences or study would help you to become more aware of various types of diversity?

A: Answers to these questions will vary with the participants' experience.

10

Effective Business Writing

THIS CHAPTER contains five types of case studies that teach various lessons about how to communicate effectively in writing. Case studies in this chapter might be used to teach skills for those who write letters and reports as well as more informal memos and electronic mail (e-mail).

See the Introduction to Part 2 on pages 63–64 for suggestions on how to select and customize the case studies in this chapter.

EFFECTIVE WRITING IDENTIFICATION CASE STUDY 37

What's Wrong?

Directions: As you read this letter to an external customer, identify what is wrong with it.

October 15, 2003

Mr. Albert Johnson
123 Main Street
Los Angeles, CA 90017

Dear Sir:

Reference is made to a telephone conversation of recent date between yourself and the undersigned, resulting from which you will please find enclosed herewith a copy of our recent computation of your premium dated September 15, 2003.

Please inform this office when the various shortages herein identified will be remedied by paying past due premiums. Only then can we think about reinstatement!

Please do not hesitate to contact this office if we can be of further assistance to answer any inquiries and expedite the reinstatement.

Very truly yours,

I. M. Neat
Individual Customer Service
Full Service Insurance Company

Facilitator Notes for Case Study 37

LEARNING OBJECTIVE: Given a case study or sample letter, identify at least five problems, errors, or mistakes that make the letter ineffective as a reader-centered message.

Possible Case Answers

These problems, errors, or mistakes include:

- Very formal outmoded tone, especially referring to oneself in the third person and change of formal tone to sarcasm by stating "Only then can we think about reinstatement!"
- Instead of "Dear Sir" address the person by name.
- First sentence is too long. An average sentence length of sixteen words is more appropriate.
- The writer uses difficult to understand words instead of simple ones that can be understood by any reader. For example, "computation" instead of "amount" or "inquiries" instead of "questions."
- Empty phrases make the meaning unclear, such as "recent date" and "herewith enclosed."

Facilitator Processing Questions and Potential Answers

Q: What makes it difficult for a reader to understand a formal letter like the one you have just read?

A: Readers find it difficult to read messages that are too formal in tone, and which use unclear language and empty phrases. If an individual is receiving bad news from a company, the reader ought to be able to identify easily what to do to fix the problem.

Q: Why is it that many people think business letters using a formal tone are appropriate?

A: Formal tone used to be required in the last century. Today, effective business writing has a less formal, yet business-like tone. Writing is more direct and clear and is written from the reader's point of view.

Q: What are some characteristics of effective business writing for reader-centered messages?

A: Characteristics of effective business writing reader-centered messages include:

- Write from the reader's point of view.
- Keep sentences short so they can be read and understood on the first reading. A recommended sixteen words per sentence length is suggested for clarity.
- Write more the way you speak to help get the right tone. Use appropriate language for the reader. A suggested guideline is 150 syllables per 100 words.
- Information is well organized and has a logical sequence for the reader.
- The purpose of the letter is clear, whether it is to inform, instruct, persuade, or document.
- Write in active voice at least 80 percent of the time. Active voice sequences parts of the sentence in this order: subject, verb, object. For example, "I refer you to our recent telephone conversation." Passive voice sequences object, verb, subject. For example, "Reference is made to a telephone conversation of recent date between yourself and the undersigned."

Q: What characteristics of effective business writing do you want to work on?

A: Answers will vary with each participant.

EFFECTIVE WRITING PROBLEM SOLVING CASE STUDY 38

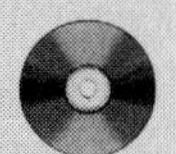

E-Mail Goes Unanswered

Directions: What might be the underlying, major problem with the e-mail in this case study? What are at least two symptoms of the problem? What are at least three suggested solutions for how to write a better e-mail message?

To: Evaluation Staff
From: Emory James, Manager
Re: Review of Proposals

It is really disappointing that none of the eight of you have met the deadline for each of you to review ten grant proposals which has come and gone with little results, since we have been charged with the responsibility to recommend which of the 80 proposals are to be funded, partially funded or refused any funding. I HAVE NO RECOMMENDATIONS FROM ANY OF YOU. THIS IS NOT ACCEPTABLE. I have heard rumors that some of you have finished your reviews, but most of you haven't even started and this assignment was given two weeks ago so the timing was not unexpected so you should have planned your time better to complete this major job assignment. Because we look bad to the Advisory Board and the City Council, as of today, all leaves and vacations are cancelled until I receive all your grant recommendations. Review the 20-page template that is attached from the USDOL that identifies criteria and how to apply the criteria to your review.

Facilitator Notes for Case Study 38

LEARNING OBJECTIVE: Given a case study or sample e-mail, identify:

- What might be the underlying, major problem with the e-mail in this case study?
- What are at least two symptoms of the problem?
- What are at least three suggested solutions for how to write a better e-mail message?

Possible Case Answers

What might be the underlying, major problem with the e-mail in this case study?

- The major problem seems to be an incomplete assignment by eight staff members. The underlying problem may have been how the assignment was given and the manager's expectations.

What are symptoms of the problem?

- None of the eight staff members have completed their assignment.
- The manager is "yelling" at the staff through capitalized words.
- The manager is reprimanding the group, and it appears that this might not be a problem for the entire group.

What are suggested solutions to writing a better e-mail message?

- Use a subject line and limit each message to that one subject area or purpose.
- Keep your message short (one screen or twenty-five lines) and concise to eliminate follow-up phone calls.
- For more than one screen, use attachments.
- Keep attachments to a minimum and size that does not overload systems and tax the patience of the reader.

- Use short paragraphs.
- Proofread each message.
- Never assume anything. Many users aren't familiar with the lingo and e-mail acronyms that you may be using.
- Avoid using all capital letters. This is the equivalent of yelling or shouting.
- Avoid making antagonizing or critical comments ("flames"). Remember e-mail is not private.

Facilitator Processing Questions and Potential Answers

Q: What makes it difficult to write a good e-mail message?

A: Many difficulties have to do with the attitude of the writer. Sometimes people write when they are upset and do not proof what is written. Others think of e-mail as a quick note and may not have the impact of a formal letter, so there is little reason to be careful with the message and how it is written. If the writer of the message acts quickly and does not proof or reconsider the tone of what is written, an inappropriate e-mail can have negative consequences.

Q: Which of the suggested solutions for better e-mail messages are easy or difficult to use?

A: Perhaps making assumptions about what the reader does or does not know is the most difficult suggestion for writing better e-mail messages. To check our assumptions means discussing them with others or having someone else read our message prior to sending it.

Q: What can you do to improve the readability of your e-mail messages?

A: Answers to this question vary with each participant.

EFFECTIVE WRITING PRACTICE CASE STUDY 39

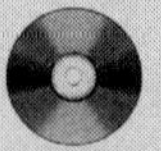

Memo to Staff

Directions: In the memo that follows, rewrite the sentences using common and specific words, and eliminate the unnecessary ones. Simplify if you can.

To All Staff Members:

Most regrettably, it has recently come to my attention that several staff members have been making frequent visitations to other floors throughout the building for the purpose of socialization with acquaintances. The lack of proximity to the work area is not conducive to good member relations.

Subsequently, such practices will be curtailed for whomsoever is involved.

Facilitator Notes for Case Study 39

LEARNING OBJECTIVE: Given a case study or sample memo, the supervisor will simplify the memo by rewriting it using common and specific words and eliminating unnecessary words.

Possible Case Answers

To All Staff Members:

Several staff members have made frequent visits to socialize with other employees on other floors. Being away from your work area is not helpful to our customers. Please be in your work area unless you are on a break.

Facilitator Processing Questions and Potential Answers

Q: What helped you rewrite the memo?

A: Writing more like one speaks helps to rewrite this type of memo. Being direct and saying what has been observed, why that is a poor practice, and what needs to be done helps the reader understand the memo.

Q: What are characteristics of well-written memos that are directing subordinates to change their behavior?

A: Characteristics of a well-written memo include the three points in the previous answer and using necessary, common, and specific words.

Q: What characteristics of well-written memos will you work on during this workshop?

A: This answer will vary by each participant.

EFFECTIVE WRITING APPLICATION CASE STUDY 40

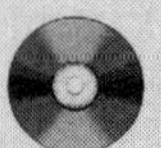

Write It Right

Directions: Usually a reader has one of three purposes in mind when reading information: to understand it, to do something with the information, or to reflect on one's attitude about the information. Different purposes in reading require different styles of writing to ensure effective writing. The following is an example of three types of writing about changing a tire on a car.

1. ***Read to understand (write for knowledge):***
   "For safety sake, when changing the tire on a car, stay out of the way of other traffic. The gearshift should be set in park and the hand brake set."
2. ***Read to do (write to direct):***
   "When changing a tire on a car, follow these safety steps before beginning to change the tire:
   - *Park the car away from the flow of traffic.*
   - *Set the gearshift in park.*
   - *Set the hand brake in park."*
3. ***Read to reflect (write to persuade):***
   "Think safety and convenience. Let our Roadside Assistance Technician change your tire for you."

Apply how to write information using three different purposes about depositing money in a checking account using an automatic teller machine (ATM). The first paragraph will inform the reader to improve an understanding of what it means to deposit money using an ATM. The second writing will direct the reader through the steps to deposit money; and the third writing encourages the reader to review the benefits of using an ATM over visiting a teller in person.

Facilitator Notes for Case Study 40

LEARNING OBJECTIVE: Given an example of three types of writing, the learner will write about depositing money using an ATM for three purposes.

Possible Case Answers

Deposit money using an ATM:

1. **Read to understand (write for knowledge):**
"Automatic tellers are a great convenience and so easy to use. They may not be friendly or smile, but they are always ready to serve you with efficiency. Deposits and withdrawals are made using an encoded plastic card."
2. **Read to do (write to direct):**
"To make a deposit using an automatic teller machine, follow these steps:
   - Place card right side up in the card slot
   - Enter personal identification code number
   - Identify the account for the transaction
   - For a deposit, enter the amount being deposited
   - Place deposit in an envelope and place envelope in slot
   - Remove card and receipt."
3. **Read to reflect (write to persuade):**
"Collect customer rewards. Use the ATM for all of your banking needs. ATMs are available 24 hours a day in convenient locations."

Facilitator Processing Questions and Potential Answers

Q: What makes it easy or difficult to write with different purposes in mind for the reader?

A: Once aware of three different purposes for the reader, it is not difficult to write any of the three styles. The difficulty may be in clarifying the reader's purpose. Some writers have difficulty writing benefit statements.

Q: What are characteristics of effective business writing for the three purposes of reading?

A: The characteristics of the three purposes of writing are

Read to understand (write for knowledge):

- Make factual statements
- Write definitions
- Explain an overview of a process in general terms

Read to do (write to direct):

- Describe the steps in a process
- Begin each step with an action verb
- Write using active voice
- List each step in the appropriate sequence

Read to reflect (write to persuade):

- Benefit statements describe "what the customer gets"
- Benefit statements show advantages of a process
- Benefit statements are intended to get someone to change their behavior

Q: How will you change your writing style to be more effective by using three different purposes for the reader?

A: Answers to this question will vary with each participant.

EFFECTIVE WRITING SERIAL CASE STUDY 41

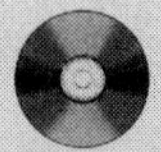

Pull It All Together

Directions: The following is a case study or example of an ineffective letter to a customer who has just purchased a new automobile. The intention of the letter is to not only congratulate the customer, but to keep the customer coming back to the dealership for all service and repairs. Correct the letter by rewriting it as a reader-centered message that uses these eight characteristics:

1. *Use common words instead of larger or less frequently understood words.*
2. *Eliminate unnecessary phrases.*
3. *Have a friendly, yet business-like tone.*
4. *Have an average sentence length of sixteen words.*
5. *Use active voice 80 percent of the message and passive voice no more than 20 percent.*
6. *Defines terms and avoids assumptions and jargon.*
7. *Have clarity and can be understood on the first reading.*
8. *Lists benefits and is written to persuade and to help the readers reflect on their attitudes.*

Dear Customer:

Thanks to customers like you for buying your new car from our dealership. Your business is greatly appreciated and it would be our pleasure to service your car and make any repairs if you have an accident. Estimates are always provided by our eminently qualified STMs before any work is done on your car and many repairs are within the warranty, so they are free! We know you were happy with our sales staff, so we know you're going to be happy using our repair and highly regarded maintenance service technicians. Your car can even be picked up for service and dropped off if your home or office is within ten miles of our dealership. Service technicians have been trained and certified by a well-known organization that trains and tests technicians so you can be sure we don't just let anybody work on your car. Come back and see us for all your service needs. We're at your disposal!

William James
Service Manager

Facilitator Notes for Case Study 41

LEARNING OBJECTIVE: Given a case study, rewrite a letter to a new car customer using eight characteristics of a reader-centered message.

Case Study Answers

Dear [use customer's name]:

Thank you for buying your new car from our dealership. We appreciate your business and would be pleased to service your car or make any repairs. Our staff of Service Technician Managers provide estimates before any work is done on your car. Many repairs are within the warranty, so they are free! We hope you were happy with our sales staff, so we know you're going to be happy using our repair and highly trained maintenance service technicians. We will pick up and drop off your car for service if your home or office is within ten miles of our dealership. Service technicians are well-trained and certified by the National Association of Automotive Repair Technicians so you can be sure of the quality of service for your automobile. Please come back and see us for all your service needs. If you call for an appointment, I know we can provide timely service.

William James
Service Manager

Facilitator Processing Questions and Potential Answers

Q: What makes it easy or difficult to write using eight characteristics of a reader-centered message?

A: Ease in using the eight characteristics of a reader-centered message comes with practice. It is often easier to edit a draft than to write the first time with all eight characteristics in mind. It is also easier to work on a few characteristics at a time than write with all eight in mind at the same time. After writing a draft, go back two or three times and edit it for different characteristics.

Q: How will you change your writing style to use all eight characteristics of effective reader-centered messages?

A: Answers to this question will vary with each participant.

11

Facilitation

THIS CHAPTER contains five types of case studies to improve skills for trainers and team leaders in group facilitation. Case studies can be used in "train-the-trainer," "quality improvement," or "meeting management" workshops.

See the Introduction to Part 2 on pages 63–64 for suggestions on how to select and customize the case studies in this chapter.

FACILITATION IDENTIFICATION CASE STUDY 42

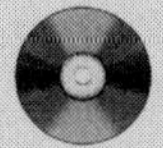

Meetings That Matter

Directions: Read the case study about Tim, a team leader in a manufacturing company who is a new facilitator. Prepare answers to these two questions: What feedback will you give Tim? What further facilitator training does Tim need?

Tim, the lead person on his shift, has been a quality improvement facilitator for six months. He attended facilitator training as part of the company's effort to make quality control everyone's job. Tim's company manufactures and distributes laboratory hardware that analyzes body fluids. The emphasis in past meetings of Tim's work group has been discussions to improve the testing and inspection process at different points of manufacture.

Tim's group has had some "quality breakthroughs." Lately, the group has developed a reputation for heated debates and does not appear as productive as it used to be. You are sitting in to observe one of Tim's group meetings. Your role is to determine what feedback or additional training Tim needs.

During the meeting you observe the following:

- Three of nine members of the group are disruptive when they arrive 15 minutes late for an hour meeting and Tim starts the meeting over.
- Tim asks the group to brainstorm ideas about an inspection problem. After 10 minutes, only three ideas are presented.
- Tim proposes groups of three develop each idea more fully. Groups of three also divide the disruptive late arrivals. Dan, a dominant member of the group, wants everyone to work on his idea. Tim gets the group to follow his directions by pointing out why he thought Dan's idea would never work.
- When each group of three reports their progress, Tim probes for details by asking, "Why do you think that will work?"

- By the end of the 60-minute meeting, two diverse ways of handling the inspection problem are being contested and defended by a divided group. Tim decides the inspection problem and proposed solutions need more investigation. He dismisses the meeting without specific assignments. Several members of the group feel things are "left up in the air" too often.

  1. What feedback will you give Tim?

  2. What further facilitator training does Tim need?

Facilitator Notes for Case Study 42

LEARNING OBJECTIVE: Given a case study, identify appropriate feedback for the facilitator and recommend further training for the facilitator.

Possible Case Answers

1. Feedback for Tim includes
   - Start and end meetings on time. If team members come late, ask one of the team members to summarize what was missed during the first part of the meeting.
   - Use techniques besides one type of brainstorming to generate additional ideas.
   - Explore options to "Why do you think that will work?" that will encourage less defensive reactions and more productive answers.
   - Don't end a meeting without closure or without identifying next steps or individual assignments.
2. Further facilitator training for Tim:
   - Creative brainstorming techniques
   - Suggestions for handling disruptive and dominant group members

Facilitator Processing Questions and Potential Answers

Q: What are essential skills for facilitators who run problem-solving team meetings?

A: These skills are essential for facilitators who run problem-solving team meetings:

- Identifying how to use different steps in a problem-solving process.

- Using a variety of brainstorming and problem-solving techniques.
- Using a variety of decision-making techniques appropriately.
- Handling dominant participants and others who disrupt the work of the team.
- Using meeting management techniques like introducing new topics, creating and using an agenda, asking questions, charting responses, testing for consensus, and so on.

Q: What are the pitfalls and problems new facilitators usually face?

A: New facilitators often allow team members to come to a conclusion too quickly. They are likely to have trouble with senior and outspoken participants.

Q: How can new facilitators overcome these pitfalls and problems?

A: Try using a variety of techniques to keep the group thinking in a divergent manner. This can include different brainstorming techniques, subgrouping, and assigning specific team members to research an issue before the next group meeting. If necessary, talk to senior participants one-on-one and enlist their support for the agenda and ask them to allow others to participate before offering their ideas.

Q: Which skills do you need to work on to improve your facilitation skills?

A: This answer will vary with the individual.

FACILITATION PROBLEM SOLVING CASE STUDY 43

Stay or Stray?

Directions: Read the following situation, and prepare these questions:

1. *Are there quick fixes?*
2. *Revisit what you want to accomplish/the objective.*
3. *Select decision-making process (self, group, default).*
4. *Review options to stay or stray from the planned course.*

It's the end of the first four-hour module of a five-module workshop. The workshop you are presenting is designed for intermediate to advanced participants. Only five of the fifteen participants can be described as intermediate or above. Several questions from the less experienced participants indicate a lack of the basics. If you continue without addressing their needs, they will be lost for the remainder of the workshop. The five more advanced participants are getting bored with the pace. They publicly complain about the slow pace up until now. You are about one hour behind where the lesson plan suggests you be at this point in the class. Attendance at this workshop is a job requirement for all fifteen participants. What will you do before ending the class and/or before the group meets for the next module?

1. Are there quick fixes?
2. Revisit what you want to accomplish/the objective.
3. Select decision-making process (self, group, default).
4. Review options to stay or stray from the planned course.

Facilitator Notes for Case Study 43

LEARNING OBJECTIVE: Given a case study, the facilitator will identify whether it is appropriate to follow or deviate from a prepared lesson plan. Provide a rationale for how you solve this problem.

Possible Case Answers

1. Quick fixes include giving an assignment to the slower participants. You can also create and distribute resource material or the option to meet with you before the next session.
2. Revisit the objectives for the course. They include successful completion of the course for all fifteen participants as a job requirement.
3. Options for deciding what to do include:
   - Making the decision yourself as the instructor.
   - Consulting with the manager of the ten deficient participants for suggestions.
   - Ignoring the situation is not an option if the objective is to be met.
4. Options to stay the course or stray from the planned course of action include:
   - Slow the pace to help the ten who are deficient.
   - Use different methods to cover basic material.
   - Give an out-of-class assignment to the ten who are deficient.
   - Provide written materials for a tutorial for the ten who are deficient.
   - Split the class into two groups and get another facilitator for one of the groups or teach the two groups yourself at different times.
   - Renegotiate the objective with the manager of the ten participants.
   - Create subgroups and have the five intermediate participants coach the ten who are deficient.

Facilitator Processing Questions and Potential Answers

Q: What makes it difficult to deal with groups when participants' experience levels are quite different?

A: Most lesson plans are written with one target population in mind. When someone outside that target population attends the training session, the pace and the activities will not meet the learning objective for all participants.

Q: What are the characteristics of appropriate options when deciding to stray from the prepared agenda for a meeting or lesson plan for a training session?

A: Appropriate strategies are those that allow the learning objective to be met. Some of the strategies in Possible Case Answers, step 4, might be appropriate if they will help all fifteen participants meet the learning objective.

Q: What will you do as a facilitator to make appropriate decisions when unexpected situations arise that could take your meeting or training session off course?

A: Answers to this question will vary by the participant.

FACILITATION PRACTICE CASE STUDIES 44, 45, AND 46

SOLVING PARTICIPANT PROBLEMS

Problem Participant Strategies

Directions: Many new and experienced facilitators have difficulty dealing with problem learners. Review the four types of problem participant strategies, and prepare answers to the case studies that follow.

Prevention Strategies

1. Inform the known disruptive participant about the subject matter **before** the session.
2. Set and agree on ground rules at the beginning of the session.
3. Know who the "question askers" are and ask for their participation before they interrupt.
4. Confront the known disruptive participants and **ask** for their help before the session.

Personal Strategies

1. Identify the **behavior** as an issue or a problem.
2. Ignore behavior that is not disruptive.
3. Recognize your own biases and stress triggers.
4. Don't take it personally.
5. Predict your success, not your failure.
6. Maintain a long-term versus short-term perspective.
7. Concentrate on reaching the group's objectives.
8. Take action to stay in control.

9. Take a break and speak to disruptive individuals privately. Ask for a behavior change before resuming the meeting.

Group Dynamics Strategies

1. Set a comfortable climate by acknowledging various points of view.
2. Ask a direct question of talkers or quiet non-participants.
3. Ask a question of the person next to the talkers or quiet non-participants.
4. Create subgroups or ask everyone to write a suggestion or point individually.
5. Acknowledge the off-track person's position and tie his/her point to the task, or have the person tie it to the task.
6. Don't get drawn into an argument; use reversed or redirected questions to move along.
7. Rescue a participant who was "shut down" by another's interruption or put-down.

Disciplinary Strategies

1. Stop talking until interrupters stop.
2. Use nonverbal cues: move closer to the disruptive people, move away from ramblers, make eye contact with side-talkers, nod your head to encourage or discourage behaviors.
3. Directly ask for silence or compliance with your directions.
4. Confront problem behavior, assertively, during or after the session. Never embarrass or put down participants.
5. Acknowledge acceptable behavior with positive reinforcement.

CASE STUDY 44

Side Conversations

Directions: Use the problem learner participant strategies and select at least one strategy from each of the four lists. Then decide which of the four strategies you selected will be most effective.

You are conducting a meeting for new managers. At the beginning of each session in the morning, after the breaks, and after lunch, two members in the rear of the room continue their side conversation several minutes into the group's meeting.

Prevention Strategy: ______________________________

Personal Strategy: ______________________________

Group Dynamics Strategy: ______________________________

Disciplinary Strategy: ______________________________

CASE STUDY 45

Space Cadet

One person in the meeting is constantly gazing into space and doodling on a piece of paper. His attention seems to drift from the subject under discussion. He has a hard time keeping up with the rest of the group.

Prevention Strategy: ______________________________

Personal Strategy: ______________________________

Group Dynamics Strategy: ______________________________

Disciplinary Strategy: ______________________________

CASE STUDY 46

Keeping the Group Together

Three people in your meeting are quite experienced managers. They seem to be way ahead of everyone else in the group. They are frequently on the next topic and having side conversations. They disrupt the rest of the group with questions that would have been unnecessary if they had been more patient.

Prevention Strategy: ______________________________

Personal Strategy: ______________________________

Group Dynamics Strategy: ______________________________

Disciplinary Strategy: ______________________________

Facilitator Notes for Case Studies 44, 45, and 46

LEARNING OBJECTIVE: Given three case studies, suggest four types of problem participant strategies that would eliminate the problem behavior while keeping the learner's self-esteem intact.

Possible Case Study Answers

Suggested answers for Case Study 44:

- Prevention strategy: set and reinforce ground rules to be sure start and ending times are clear.
- Personal strategy: don't take it personally, and concentrate on reaching the group's objectives.
- Group dynamics strategy: create subgroups or ask everyone to write a suggestion or point individually. Ask a question of the person next to the talkers.
- Disciplinary strategy: stop talking until interrupters stop or move closer to the disruptive people.

Suggested answers for Case Study 45:

- Prevention strategy: as a ground rule, suggest everyone has an obligation to participate in group discussions.
- Prevention strategy: ignore this non-disruptive behavior or take a break and speak to the individual personally.
- Group dynamics strategy: ask a direct question of this person to determine the source of confusion.
- Disciplinary strategy: move closer to this person or make eye contact if possible.

Suggested answers for Case Study 46:

- Prevention strategy: set and agree on staying with the group as a ground rule.

- Personal strategy: don't take it personally, or take a break to speak privately with the three experienced managers.
- Group dynamics strategy: subgroup, and be sure to divide the three experienced managers.
- Disciplinary strategy: move closer to the disruptive managers.

Facilitator Processing Questions and Potential Answers

Q: Which type of strategy has the greatest risk? Which has the lowest risk?

A: Disciplinary strategies have the greatest risk of alienating the entire group. The lowest risk strategies are prevention, personal, and group dynamics strategies.

Q: If you use more than one strategy, what is an appropriate sequence of strategies?

A: When the facilitator is in the midst of running a group meeting, try the group dynamics strategies. Plan for the next meeting using prevention strategies. If needed, try taking a break or use some of the personal strategies. Starting with disciplinary strategies leaves the facilitator with no additional options if that strategy fails. Starting with a group dynamics strategy leaves open the opportunity to take a break and use a personal strategy or use a disciplinary strategy.

Q: Which of these strategies is easiest to use? Which is the most difficult for you to use?

A: Answers will vary with individuals.

FACILITATION APPLICATION CASE STUDY 47

Facilitate Meetings with Ease

Directions: Read the list of ten facilitation skills, then identify which skills the facilitator in the case study applies well and what he can do to improve the effectiveness of these techniques.

Ten Facilitation Techniques

1. Initiate, propose, and make suggestions.
2. Divide into subgroups.
3. Use questioning to draw people out, and elicit information and opinions.
4. Use silence to make space.
5. Keep track of multiple topics and build on the ideas of others.
6. Use flip charting to generate additional discussion and record ideas.
7. Listen for common themes, bar irrelevant details, and redirect discussion.
8. Organize the sequence of speakers.
9. Paraphrase to clarify or show understanding.
10. Have group members relate specific examples to a general idea or make a summary.

Tim, the lead person on his shift, has been a quality improvement facilitator for a year. He attended facilitator training as part of the company's effort to make quality control everyone's job. After some difficult team meetings in the first six months, Tim's group has come together to solve most of its problems. Tim's company manufactures and distributes laboratory hardware that analyzes body fluids. The emphasis in past meetings of Tim's work group has been discussions to improve the testing and inspection process at different points of manufacture. The group has successfully implemented a number of improvements. The current discussion is about formalizing a troubleshooting process that all team members will use. Team members at today's meeting include:

- Barbara, the newest technician and recent college graduate
- Paulo, a senior technician with the most seniority at the company
- Nhung, an experienced technician without formal education and a natural at problem solving, software issues, and troubleshooting
- Dan, a dominant and outspoken technician who resents not being the team leader

Tim: "OK, let's get started. We have a partially completed troubleshooting flowchart on the board. I'd like to finish the process charting in the next hour. This is the only item on our agenda. How does that sound to the rest of you?"

Dan: "I guess that's OK; but I think you have a problem at point five on the chart. We ought to fix that before we try to finish the rest of the process."

Tim: "Dan, that's not my memory of how we ended last time. If you have some suggestions about point five, we can start there. Any other suggestions?"

Barbara: "Tim, do you want me to chart and take notes during the meeting?"

Tim: "Yes, thanks Barbara. You did a great job at the last meeting capturing everyone's ideas. Here are copies of Barbara's notes from the last meeting." (Tim distributes notes from the last meeting.)

Paulo: "Dan's right. We will be more successful if we fix point five first. I've been thinking about it and drew up two options for it. Let me show it to you and see what the rest of you think."

(Paulo explains his suggestion for the next five minutes. Paulo answers questions from the rest of the group. Tim has not offered any comments and only organized the sequence of speakers when more than one team member wanted to speak at the same time. Barbara is charting questions and summarizes points in writing for all to see.)

Tim: "Nhung, you've come up with an interesting change to what Paulo is suggesting. What do the rest of you think about it?"
(The others concur with Nhung's suggested change.)

Tim: "Barbara, you've been pretty quiet so far. It looks like you're getting all this down. Do you have any questions? I don't want you to feel left out."

Barbara: "No, I don't have any questions. Much of what you are discussing is similar to what I studied in school. It's interesting to see what goes on in the real world. It's intimidating to see how theoretical much of my academic work has been. Here, we see how what we do affects the test on real patients. When I completed lab work at school, fluids were made up numbers since we were never working with real patients and our software makes the process much easier than the manual troubleshooting we had to do."

Tim: "Barbara, now that we have fixed point five, what do you think the next step ought to be in the troubleshooting process?"

Barbara: "Well, I'm not sure but my guess is we need to divide the field in half and begin testing at critical junction points."

Nhung: "Good guess, Barbara. You did learn something in school, but I see one software issue none of us have addressed."

Tim: "Let's summarize what we have so far and then we'll look at the software issue."

(Nhung makes a summary from Barbara's charting. Tim asks for consensus and the group agrees after some discussion of a minor point.)

Tim: "We're just about out of time. I'm disappointed we didn't finish the process today. However, we did refine the process and we all agree on it so far. Nhung, would you send us an e-mail with the software issue? I'd like the rest of you to consider it before we meet again on Friday. Dan and Paulo, I'd like the two of you to meet before Friday and develop a draft of the rest of the process. Your two options on point five really helped us today."

Identify which of the ten skills Tim, the facilitator in the case study, applies well and what he can do to improve the effectiveness of these techniques.

Facilitator Notes for Case Study 47

LEARNING OBJECTIVE: Given a case study and ten facilitation techniques, the learner will identify how a facilitator applies each technique and make suggestions where application falls short.

Possible Case Answers

Here are the ten facilitation techniques. Table 11.1 shows what Tim does well and what he can do to improve.

Table 11.1. Facilitation Techniques for Case Study 47.

Technique	*What Was Done Well*	*What He Can Do to Improve*
Initiate, propose, and make suggestions	He gets the group off to a good start and summarizes.	He could have handed out the notes from the last meeting sooner. He didn't wait for a response from the group before ending the meeting.
Divide into subgroups	This is done at the end and might work well.	Tim could have used this technique during the meeting to accomplish more.
Use questioning to draw people out, and elicit information and opinions	This worked well with Barbara.	Dan was ignored for most of the meeting.
Use silence to make space	Not able to observe.	
Keep track of multiple topics and build on the ideas of others	Tim seemed to do well by keeping the agenda, diverting to point five and pulling the group back together.	

Table 11.1. Facilitation Techniques for Case Study 47 (Continued).

Technique	*What Was Done Well*	*What He Can Do to Improve*
Use flip charting to generate additional discussion and record ideas	Tim had Barbara record ideas.	Be sure a designated recorder captures all ideas and not just personal views.
Listen for common themes, bar irrelevant details, and redirect discussion	Tim was accepting of ideas from others.	Tim was unable to reach the objective of the meeting.
Organize the sequence of speakers	Tim did this well.	
Paraphrase to clarify or show understanding	He acknowledges and thanks others, but doesn't actually paraphrase.	Paraphrasing the ideas of others would improve clarity and understanding.
Have group members relate specific examples to a general idea or make a summary	This seems to flow well in the meeting without much direction from Tim. He also asks others to make a summary, which is an inclusive behavior.	

Facilitator Processing Questions and Potential Answers

Q: Which of the ten techniques seems the easiest for this facilitator to apply?

A: The techniques that seem easiest to use are

- Initiate, propose, and make suggestions
- Divide into subgroups

- Keep track of multiple topics and build on the ideas of others
- Use flip charting to generate additional discussion and record ideas
- Organize the sequence of speakers
- Have group members relate specific examples to a general idea or make a summary

Q: Which of the ten techniques seems the most difficult for this facilitator to apply?

A: The techniques that seem the most difficult to use are

- Use questions to draw people out, and elicit information and options
- Listen for common themes, bar irrelevant details, and redirect discussion
- Paraphrase to clarify or show understanding

Q: What makes these techniques more difficult to apply?

A: These three techniques are more difficult because it requires the facilitator to have great awareness and track contributions by everyone. While listening, the facilitator must judge the contributions of others and paraphrase them for clarity. It does require thinking and doing more than one thing at a time.

Q: What are the benefits of using facilitation techniques, even though they might be difficult to apply?

A: The benefit of using these facilitation techniques is to encourage the group to participate and offer ideas. The key role of a facilitator is to meet the objective and involve the best thinking of the group.

Q: Which facilitation techniques do you need to work on to gain the benefits identified in the previous question?

A: Answers to this question will vary with each learner.

Facilitation Serial Case Study

Each of the four case studies in this chapter addresses a different aspect of facilitation for the same team. Tim, the facilitator, seems to develop new skills with each case study. Taken together, each case study can build upon each other to be used as a serial case study. The first case helps a facilitator identify effective meeting facilitation techniques. The second case helps a facilitator make measured decisions to stay with an agenda or stray from it. The third case helps a facilitator handle problem participant behaviors using four distinct strategies and a variety of tactics. The fourth case study helps a facilitator apply ten meeting facilitation techniques. After using all four of these case studies, ask the Facilitator Processing Questions.

Facilitator Processing Questions and Potential Answers

Q: What have you learned about effective meeting facilitation from these four case studies?

Q: What barriers do you face in using the meeting facilitation techniques suggested in these case studies?

Q: How will you overcome these barriers?

Q: Which of these facilitation techniques require further development for you to feel more comfortable facilitating meetings?

Q: How will you continue your development as a facilitator?

A: Answers to these questions will vary with each participant.

12

Influencing

THIS CHAPTER contains five types of case studies that teach various lessons about how to influence others. Influencing skills can be used to influence decisions and actions taken by others. Others can be peers, subordinates, or higher than you in a reporting relationship. Case studies in this chapter might be used in "leadership," "communication," or "selling skills" classes.

See the Introduction to Part 2 on pages 63–64 for suggestions on how to select and customize the case studies in this chapter.

INFLUENCING IDENTIFICATION CASE STUDY 48

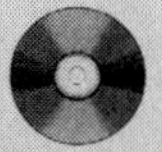

How to Get Results

Directions: For each of the following three case studies, identify what influencing style would be most appropriate and effective. Choose your influencing style from these three alternatives: supportive, directive, problem solving. Supportive influencing is defined as being helpful, non-threatening, and comforting. Directive influencing is defined as giving an expert opinion or requiring others to do as you ask. Problem-solving influencing is non-threatening by offering reasoned options through an inclusive and consulting style.

1. You are a trainer who is teaching a workshop for new employees who don't seem to have much of a work ethic. One of the employees is complaining about a problem she is having with an assignment. She has been having difficulty getting to class on time, with her new childcare giver, her child has been sick and she missed a day at school, she couldn't afford to fill the child's prescription, on and on.
   - What is your role?
   - Which style of influencing would be most effective? Why?
2. You are a social worker who reviews safety and childcare services of 100 providers in your county. One of your responsibilities is to visit childcare providers to be sure regulations are being followed and at least the minimums of services are offered. During a home visit, a childcare provider is reluctant to spend observation time with you so she can be trained to interact appropriately with children. This is your third visit and you have repeatedly asked the provider to remain in the room while you model reading to the children and appropriate child interaction. She once again sees your arrival as an opportunity for a welcome break from caring for the children.
   - What is your role?
   - Which style of influencing would be most effective? Why?

3. You are conducting a workshop that requires learners to pass an end-of-course test as a job requirement. A student in your workshop complains about a recent unit test you gave saying that three questions were confusing and she would have received a passing grade if the questions had been clearer. Other students in the class agree with the complaint. One student recommends you just throw out the whole test.

   - What is your role?
   - Which style of influencing would be most effective? Why?

Facilitator Notes for Case Study 48

LEARNING OBJECTIVE: Given a case study, the learner will identify a comfortable influencing style for a given situation that will bring the desired result.

Possible Case Answers

1. Your role is to get the new employee to complete an assignment on time and try to influence her to have a more positive attitude. The influencing style that might be most effective in this situation is "supportive." A supportive influencing style would show empathy for the new employee's problems while refocusing on results.
2. Your role is to get the childcare worker to accept your visits as an opportunity to be trained in providing services, such as reading to children. A "directive" style might be most appropriate since the childcare worker does not seem to understand her role during your visit is to learn how to deliver a new service, not take a break. Clearly explain the purpose of the visit and tell the childcare worker to remain in the room. After you model how to read to children and demonstrate appropriate interaction with the children, ask the childcare worker to give a return demonstration of those two skills while you observe her.
3. Your role is to help the students gain skill and demonstrate their competence by passing an end-of-course test. A "problem solving" influencing style might be the most appropriate style in this situation. There seem to be three confusing questions on the test that could produce different results if they were more clearly worded. Be careful to define the problem narrowly and not lose the integrity of the testing process.

Facilitator Processing Questions and Potential Answers

Q: What factors help you decide which influencing style is more appropriate?

A: Consider three factors when trying to decide which influencing style might be the most effective in a given situation:

- Your preference for one style that is most comfortable, given your personality.
- The situation itself may suggest that one style may be more successful than another.
- How decisions are made in your organization's culture may suggest one style over another. For example, if management is open to suggestions and encourages participative decision making, a directive style can be appropriate if you are an expert in a subject and someone in authority wants your opinion. If you are unable to influence an outcome, being supportive and understanding might be the only style possible.

Q: What problems can result from using the wrong influencing style?

A: If you use the wrong influencing style you might appear to be pushy, authoritative, weak, or indecisive.

Q: Which influencing style is most comfortable for you to use?

A: Answers will vary with each participant.

Q: What are the advantages and disadvantages of your most comfortable influencing style?

A: Advantages and disadvantages of each influencing style are shown in Table 12.1:

Table 12.1. Influencing Styles: Advantages and Disadvantages.

Influencing Style	*Advantages*	*Disadvantages*
Supportive	• Non-threatening • Comforting when taking direction is difficult • When you are not an expert	• May be seen as sympathetic rather than decisive • Can be misread as a weakness
Directive	• Easy for an expert • Often accepted by others who are aware of your expertise	• When others need to feel a solution is theirs • When others are wrong and your ideas challenge them
Problem Solving	• Non-threatening • Convinces others when they can follow your reasoning • Appropriate for staff people and influencing upward in the organization	• When issues are emotional rather than rational • When someone is asking for advice rather than analysis

Q: How can you become more comfortable in using another influencing style in the right situation?

A: Answers will vary with each participant.

INFLUENCING PROBLEM SOLVING CASE STUDY 49

Just Say "No"

Directions: Using your influence appropriately sometimes means getting others to change their minds or refusing a request. Read the case study, and identify the problem. What would you do in this situation?

You are sitting in your office on Friday afternoon. You already have more work than you can handle. Now your manager walks in and tells you, "Look, I know you're loaded down with several projects, but I need this one finished by Monday morning. I wish I could give you more time, but the VP is really hot on this. You've always come through for me before. I know I can depend on you." You already have weekend commitments that you are reluctant to break.

- What is the problem?
- What are the symptoms of the problem?
- What do you do?

Facilitator Notes for Case Study 49

LEARNING OBJECTIVE: After reading this case, the learner will identify why it is difficult to say "no" to a boss and identify options to resolve the underlying problem, rather than treat symptoms.

Possible Case Answers

What is the problem? The manager has failed to give a subordinate enough notice to handle a priority project.

What are the symptoms of the problem?

- The subordinate already has several projects.
- The manager waited until the last minute, making it difficult for the subordinate to say "no."
- The manager is intruding into the employee's personal time.

What do you do?

- First of all, don't assume the best or only way to handle this problem is to cancel personal plans for the weekend.
- Reprioritize existing projects in light of this new assignment.
- Seek assistance from others who could help the manager meet the deadline.
- Acknowledge that you are a "dependable" person.
- Clarify the manager's expectations about the tasks that absolutely need to be done and the time of the deadline on Monday morning.
- Tell the manager what you can do within work hours.
- Ask for approval to work overtime.

Facilitator Processing Questions

Q: Why is it difficult for some people to say "no"?

A: Why is it difficult for some people to say "no"?

- Most people don't realize there are many ways to say "no." For example, you can offer partial assistance, make compromises, ask for clarification before agreeing to do any part of the task.
- If you are a dependable person, you may have encouraged others to seek your compliance with unreasonable demands by past behavior.
- The manager is a superior and you may not feel you have the right to refuse this request.
- The request might be a demand disguised as a request.

Q: What are circumstances or situations when you find it difficult to say "no"?

A: Individual answers will vary with each participant.

Q: Which of the options to saying "no" might work for you?

A: Individual answers will vary with each participant.

Q: When trying to influence another, why is it beneficial to sort the symptoms from the root causes of a problem?

A: You are more likely to be influential when addressing root causes. By addressing symptoms of an issue or problem, you are likely to be distracted "fixing" peripheral issues and lose an opportunity to influence the real decision maker.

Q: What gets in the way of identifying the root cause of a problem?

A: Sometimes unclear thinking, emotional issues, or personal agendas get in the way of identifying root problems. Root problems may also be threatening or too difficult to resolve. Those who adapt an avoidance style of dealing with difficult issues rarely attack root causes of problems.

INFLUENCING PRACTICE CASE STUDY 50

Influencing Through Questions

Directions: Often you can influence others by aligning your request with the other person's beliefs and values. If you sense disagreement, asking open-ended questions can help you understand the other person's beliefs and values. As you read the case study, look for facts you can confirm, beliefs or opinions of those involved, and underlying values (desires, wants) of the claims manager and claims processors. Then write open-ended questions to clarify beliefs and values.

The disability insurance claims manager has been told to reduce the average time it takes to process a claim by 10 percent. The claims manager tells the processors they will need to come up with a more efficient way to process claims in the department. The claims manager is under pressure to do more with less.

The claims processors think this search for efficiency is a waste of time and there is little room for improvement inside the department. The processors admit they are doing some duplicate work and a few efficiencies can be achieved here. Waiting for information from the insured and/or the investigators who do not provide claim and policy information in a timely manner causes most of the delays.

The manager is hesitant to put pressure on customers or investigators because he thinks this could slow things down even more.

1. Identify the facts, beliefs, and values stated here by the claims manager.
2. What open questions would you ask of the claims manager?
3. Identify facts, beliefs, and values stated by the claims processors.
4. What questions would you ask of the claims processors?

Facilitator Notes for Case Study 50

LEARNING OBJECTIVE: Given a case study, the participants will be able to ask open-ended questions to learn more about the beliefs and values of the other person in order to increase their influence.

Possible Case Answers

1. Identify the facts, beliefs, and values stated here by the claims manager.
   - Facts: The manager has been told to reduce processing time for a claim by 10 percent. Waiting for information causes delays.
   - Beliefs: The processors can come up with efficiencies. Pressure on customers and investigators would slow processing time even more.
   - Values: Doing more with less is desirable.
2. What open questions would you ask of the claims manager?
   - What kinds of efficiencies do you think are possible for the processors?
   - How could we encourage customers and investigators to provide more timely claim and policy information?
   - What are other sources for claim and policy information that could speed up the process?
3. Identify facts, beliefs, and values stated by the claims processors.
   - Facts: There is duplicate work being done inside the department.
   - Beliefs: There is little room for improvement inside the department. Customers and investigators cause most of the delays.
   - Values: Wasting time is bad.
4. What questions would you ask of the claims processors?
   - How could duplicate work inside the department be eliminated?
   - How much processing time would that save?

- Even though there seems to be little room for improvement inside the department, what suggestions do you have for reducing processing time?
- What would encourage customers and investigators to respond more promptly?
- What other efficiencies can you recommend?

Facilitator Processing Questions and Potential Answers

Q: What were the differences in how the facts of the case are seen by either side?

A: Facts are facts and the only difference may be in the facts a particular side chooses to recognize, especially if it helps prove their point.

Q: After asking open-ended questions, do you think you will have enough information to accurately identify the beliefs and values of the other person?

A: You ought to be able to get enough information to influence the other party. If not, ask more questions.

Q: How can aligning what you want the other person to do with their beliefs and values achieve the results you want?

A: Most people act out of self-interest so if you can show the other person the benefits of what you want them to do by aligning it with their beliefs and values, you are more likely to get the results you desire. Beliefs can be influenced with evidence that supports a different opinion. However, values are more deeply held desires and often personal, so rather than trying to get the other person to change what they value, honoring another's values will avoid conflict.

INFLUENCING APPLICATION CASE STUDY 51

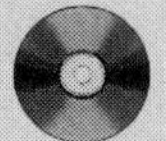

Influencing Decision Makers

Directions: If you want to influence decisions makers, identify how others make decisions and what type of information is persuasive for this person. Different decision makers need different types of information. Five typical types of persuasive information include:

1. ***Testimonials*** *tell the decision maker about your satisfied customers. They are written endorsements.*
2. ***References*** *are individuals that the decision maker can contact and discuss specific issues with them.*
3. ***Research*** *shows results achieved by applying a similar strategy to a similar situation and hoping for similar results.*
4. ***A pilot program*** *offers a program or a solution for a small group with the hope that the same solution can be applied successfully on a wider basis.*
5. ***Cost-benefit analysis*** *demonstrates the savings or return to the organization for an expenditure.*

For the case study that follows, identify what type of influencing strategy or strategies might persuade the decision maker to select your preferred option. Be prepared to discuss your rationale for selecting each type of influencing strategy.

Last week you heard a really dynamic speaker on "Overcoming Resistance to Change" at a professional association luncheon. It sparked an idea. You have since read two or three articles on the subject. You believe you have found the key to making the county government agency you are working with more effective at implementing a new computerized control system. Since you have worked with the agency management for years and know this group well, this speaker would be perfect for a satellite-training event in six months. As you put together a plan of action to recommend this speaker for the training in six months, what type of persuasive information would get your plan approved?

Facilitator Notes for Case Study 51

LEARNING OBJECTIVE: Given a case study and five types of influencing strategies, the learner will recognize the most effective application of each strategy.

Possible Case Answers

Here are the five types of influencing strategies and an analysis of whether each would persuade a decision maker in this case:

1. **Testimonials** from others would probably not influence the decision maker as much as your personal recommendation.
2. **References** from you might be helpful. Try to find additional references where another government agency has used this speaker and achieve a positive result.
3. **Research** might be helpful. Ask the company installing the new computer control software as well as those in your county's Information Technology group about their experience in successfully reducing resistance to this type of implementation.
4. **A pilot program** in this case would be hiring this speaker to work with one small group in the County who will be implementing the software changes. If resistance to the software changes works in the pilot group, it might help in having a wider group trained, possibly through a satellite-delivered workshop.
5. **Cost-benefit analysis** would persuade those who would pay for such a program. When developing a cost-benefit analysis for soft skills training, it is not always easy to quantify how resistance to a software installation could affect the county's bottom line. If a training expenditure were to help the project stay within its budget, then using a cost-benefit analysis might be persuasive.

Facilitator Processing Questions and Potential Answers

Q: What makes it easy or difficult to come up with an appropriate influencing strategy that will persuade a decision maker?

A: The more experience and contact you have had with a particular decision maker, the easier it may be to predict which strategy is most likely to be successful.

Q: What are the advantages and disadvantages of each of the five strategies?

A: See the table below for the advantages and disadvantages of each of the five influencing strategies.

Table 12.2. Influencing Strategies: Advantages and Disadvantages.

Influencing Strategy	*Advantages*	*Disadvantages*
Testimonials	Evidence that someone likes your idea	Only helpful if testimonial comes from a credible person
References	Need to be specific to your industry and for a specific idea, person, or program	If not current and specific references are not helpful
Research	Helpful if specifically matched to a specific idea, person, or program	Difficult to find credible research for some topics
Pilot	Direct proof the program or idea will work in your organization	Sometimes difficult to create a group that is typical of the entire target population
Cost-benefit analysis	Will convince those who approve expenditures	Sometimes difficult to develop "hard" numbers for "soft" skills

Q: What types of influencing strategies will help you influence decision makers in your organization?

A: Answers will vary with each participant. Encourage participants to explain the rationale for their decisions.

INFLUENCING SERIAL CASE STUDY 52

Is Retraining the Answer?

Directions: Read the case study, and progressively identify:

1. *The type of influencing style appropriate for this situation: supportive, directive, or problem solving.*
2. *Define the problem, major symptoms of the problem, and a plan of action.*
3. *What are the facts of the case? What are the beliefs and values of the head teller?*
4. *Which of the five types of strategies will work best to resolve this issue?*

You manage a teller training school for a major commercial bank. You have been hearing rumors that one of your teller trainers is teaching a process differently than how the process is being done in the two branches you visited last week. You have been unable to observe this part of the lesson. Two weeks after what appeared to have been a successful class, a head teller confronts you during your branch visit. She lists the areas she had to conduct retraining for the new tellers who were in the latest class. She resents wasting her time this way. She had to make two embarrassing calls to customers to explain the problems that were caused by incorrectly completed processes and how the problems had been corrected. Answer the four questions in the directions.

Facilitator Notes for Case Study 52

LEARNING OBJECTIVE: Given the same case study, develop a complete influencing strategy by identifying the appropriate influencing style and strategy for this situation along with a complete statement of the problem, symptoms, and plan of action.

Possible Case Answers

1. The type of influencing style appropriate for this situation is problem solving.
2. Define the problem: different processes are taught at the teller school and in the branch. Major symptoms of the problem are complaints and rumors of complaints. A plan of action includes interviewing head tellers from several branches and reviewing material presented at the teller school to identify discrepancies. Changes can be made to the training or other solutions presented, based on what is discovered during the interviews.
3. The facts of the case include rumors, complaints, and you not being available to observe a workshop. The head teller believes the teller trainers are teaching more than one process incorrectly and she needs to retrain employees who attend teller training. The head teller values productivity and deplores situations that waste her time and the time of her subordinates. The head teller also values customer relationships as evidenced by her actions to correct a processing problem.
4. As for which of the five types of strategies will work best to resolve this issue, that will depend on what is uncovered during the branch interviews with head tellers. If the teller school is teaching a process incorrectly, the head teller who told you about the problem might be a good resource to pilot changes in the workshop. If you need to cost-justify the expense of course redesign to higher management,

completing a cost-benefit analysis would be useful. Testimonials, references, and research strategies do not seem appropriate for resolution of this problem.

Facilitator Processing Questions and Potential Answers

Q: What aspect of influencing is most helpful to you in your organization?

Q: What aspect of influencing do you need to work on to influence decision-makers in your organization?

Q: How might you continue to develop your influencing style and apply appropriate influencing strategies?

A: Answers for the three questions will vary with each participant.

13

Needs Assessment

THIS CHAPTER contains five types of case studies that teach various lessons about how to conduct a variety of needs assessments. Managers, supervisors, and trainers conduct needs assessments to learn more about whether there is a training issue, or to learn information about a target population so a training program can be designed appropriately to meet their needs. Needs assessments are also conducted to break down a job or a task so it can be taught to others. Needs assessments can be a formal process when using a survey instrument or written questionnaire, or an informal process involving a series of interviews. Case studies in this chapter might be used in "leadership, supervisor, management" or "train-the-trainer" classes.

See the Introduction to Part 2 on pages 63–64 for suggestions on how to select and customize the case studies in this chapter.

NEEDS ASSESSMENT IDENTIFICATION CASE STUDY 53

Going Downhill

Directions: As you read about the deteriorating performance of Sharon, identify what's gone wrong.

During the past few years there has been much emphasis on quality service and staff development along with many dynamic changes at Alliance Skilled Nursing Facility (ASNF). It has become an even more exciting environment now that the new emphasis is mission, margin, and occupancy. Most of the employees are excited about the changes and the opportunities to be creative to meet and exceed our goals.

One of your team leaders, Sharon, has been at ASNF for 8 years. She is a skilled administrator and, in the past, you have been able to count on her to provide excellent mentoring (training) to new staff. For the last year or so, you have been noticing an increasing amount of negative talk and seeing a change in the way Sharon relates to others on the job (other administrators, staff, and yourself). She seems to you to be quite cynical. She voices skepticism about changes, often saying things like "I'll believe it when I see it" or "the company doesn't support us, it just keeps giving us more to do and more expectations that can't be met."

She has complained loudly to you and to others on the team about the training efforts for the new administrators: "We never put that kind of money into training when I became an administrator. We're just spoonfeeding them. Either they have it or they don't." She seems to be focused on past history and evaluates the current advancements and changes based on actions from the past.

Sharon's last two performance reviews have been reflective of these changes. It's not so much that she's not doing the job, it's that she's *just doing the job* and no more. The reviews have not reflected her high level of competency, because her performance has not demonstrated it. This has seemed to decrease Sharon's motivation even further.

You are becoming increasingly concerned about two issues: that Sharon's performance will continue to deteriorate and that her behavior will influence the attitudes of the rest of the team, particularly new administrators.

What's gone wrong for Sharon?

Facilitator Notes for Case Study 53

LEARNING OBJECTIVE: Given a case study, the manager will identify at least three things that have gone wrong for this once high-performing employee.

Possible Case Answers

A number of things seem to have gone "wrong" for Sharon:

- The organization has formalized its mission, margin, and occupancy goals and Sharon does not seem excited about the goals like her co-workers and has not voiced her specific concerns about the changes.
- Sharon is talking negatively and is quite critical and skeptical about the changes.
- She is critical about the cost of training for new administrators and sees it as a "spoonfeeding" approach.
- Sharon is doing the minimum to get by on fulfilling job requirements. She is working below her high level of competency.
- Critical reviews further discourage Sharon.
- Sharon's behavior is negatively influencing the team, and new administrators in particular.

Facilitator Processing Questions and Potential Answers

Q: What makes it easy or difficult to identify poor performance issues from a written summary as seen in this case study?

A: If a case is simple and enough information is provided, it is easy to identify poor performance issues. However, very few poor performance issues are ever as simple as portrayed in a case study.

Q: How can you more clearly identify the number and depth of issues in this case?

A: Asking questions of enough people involved in the issues can lead to a greater understanding about the number and depth of issues. Systematic approaches have been developed to ask appropriate questions. Works by Robert Mager and Dana Gaines Robinson are suggested in the bibliography of this book.

Q: The first step in resolving poor performance is to identify the issues. What are the other steps you need to take to assess the needs in this case thoroughly?

A: Additional steps to identifying issues are to:

- Sort issues into those you are capable of addressing and those you are not.
- Classify issues as having to do with knowledge, skill, or attitude so appropriate solutions will be sought.
- Validate the issues from at least one other point of view.
- Get statistical and anecdotal information, if possible.
- Proceed with the next problem-solving steps.

Q: How would you sort the issues you discovered so far into issues around lack of knowledge, lack of skill, or poor attitude?

A: Many of the issues described in the case study answers seem to have an emotional or "attitude" component. It could be that additional information would change Sharon's mind and influence her attitude. There are so few issues that are skill-based. She could perform better if she wanted to.

NEEDS ASSESSMENT PROBLEM SOLVING CASE STUDY 54

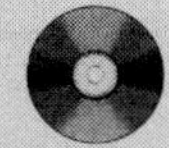

Damage Control

Directions: As you read the case study, identify the problem and whom you would like to interview to uncover all dimensions of the problem. What questions will you ask during these interviews?

The Director of Public Relations and Fund Raising at Community Medical Center has asked you to present a "Guest Relations Workshop" for all employees who have patient contact.

The Director has described the Emergency Room employees as a particularly "needy" group for this type of training. He suggests their lack of normal "social graces" and a few cases of "burn out" are giving the Medical Center a bad reputation and making it difficult to raise funds in the community.

Just last week, Mrs. Richbucks, a significant benefactor for the Medical Center, had to wait several hours for treatment of a minor but painful injury. The wait was quite uncomfortable and she was all but forgotten by the insensitive staff.

1. Who would you want to interview besides the Director of Public Relations and Fund Raising?
2. What questions will you ask of the Director and others to uncover all dimensions of the real problem?

Facilitator Notes for Case Study 54

LEARNING OBJECTIVE: Given a case study, the learner will ask enough questions to uncover all the dimensions of a problem.

Possible Case Answers

1. Interviewing the Emergency Room Supervisor as well as the Emergency Room employees would be appropriate. Interviewing Mrs. Richbucks might produce interesting information, but talking with her would be at the discretion of the Director of Public Relations and Fund Raising.
2. Questions for the Director and others include:
   - How typical was the wait experienced by Mrs. Richbucks in the Emergency Room?
   - What are past indicators of satisfactory or unsatisfactory performance in the Emergency Room? Is this incident counter to current satisfaction trends?
   - What is the intake process in the Emergency Room? Was that process followed when Mrs. Richbucks was there?
   - What occurred in the Emergency Room that impacted levels of service and waiting time?
   - What are Emergency Room employees doing that demonstrates Guest Relations training is needed?

Facilitator Processing Questions and Potential Answers

Q: What do you notice about how these questions are asked?

A: The questions are open-ended and worded to gain lots of information. They do not lead the other person and allow the answerer to proceed in any direction that is appropriate.

Q: What are other problem-solving steps that could be used to gather more information related to these issues?

A: Customer or patient satisfaction surveys might reveal whether the incident with Mrs. Richbucks was typical or an anomaly. Other Medical Center managers who interface with the Emergency Room could be interviewed.

Q: What types of questions do you need to develop to become more proficient at needs assessments?

A: Answers will vary with each participant.

NEEDS ASSESSMENT PRACTICE CASE STUDY 55

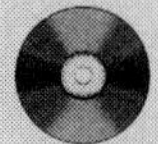

Is This a Sweet Deal?

Directions: Review the following situation, and identify what information Pete needs to develop through a needs assessment before presenting the vice president with a cost-effective solution to their personnel issues.

Pete is the training coordinator at Sweet Life Inc., a fast-growing chain of retail candy shops. The shops are located in large malls and offer a variety of "homemade"-type sweets. Each shop has at least four people on shift during store hours. There is a manager and three staff people who cook, clean, and sell.

The Vice President (VP) of Store Operations is concerned about the quality of store personnel that are recruited, interviewed, oriented, and trained in a variety of demanding tasks. All of these tasks and more fall on the already burdened shoulders of the store manager. After several discussions with the VP of Store Operations, Pete's first thought is to improve the interviewing skills of store managers. This type of training would help the quality of store personnel hired by the store managers. Pete has the VP's approval to work toward a solution, but keep the cost down.

1. What is the purpose or objective of conducting a needs assessment?
2. What type of information does Pete need to develop before proceeding with interviewing skills training?
3. Who should he ask?
4. What questions should he ask?

Facilitator Notes for Case Study 55

LEARNING OBJECTIVE: Given a case study, the learner will identify the type of information that needs to be developed and identify questions to develop that information.

Possible Case Answers

1. The purpose of the needs assessment is to identify how to improve the quality of store personnel that are recruited, interviewed, oriented, and trained.
2. What type of information does Pete need to develop before proceeding with interviewing skills training?
   - What are the current recruitment and hiring practices?
   - What are the VP's concerns about the quality of store personnel?
   - What is the cause of quality deficiencies?
   - To what extent are store managers burdened, and how does this affect the recruitment, hiring, orienting, and training of new employees?
   - How would skills training in interviewing improve the situation?
3. Who should he ask?
   - VP of Operations
   - Selected Store Managers
4. What questions should he ask?
   - How are job candidates recruited?
   - How effective are recruitment methods?
   - What other recruitment avenues might produce a better group of job candidates?

- How often do you need to interview job candidates to fill openings?
- How protracted is the interviewing process to get a qualified candidate?
- What prevents you from conducting a quality interview with a job candidate?
- How do you prepare to interview a job candidate?
- What legal guidelines do you follow to be sure you ask appropriate questions?
- What do you do to orient a new employee?
- What basic training do you provide for new employees in your store?
- What types of training would help you recruit, interview, orient, and train your new employees?

Facilitator Processing Questions and Potential Answers

Q: What makes it easy or difficult to go through the discipline of a needs assessment when your instincts point you toward an obvious solution?

A: It might appear difficult to go through the discipline of conducting a needs assessment and uncovering all the dimensions of an issue. This is especially true when your boss is demanding quick answers and wants to keep costs down. However, it is easier to do the needs assessment first than to retract your steps after the "obvious solution" fails and you need to start over.

Q: What concerns do you have about widening the people involved in developing information for the assessment?

A: The more people involved, the longer it takes to get to a decision about how the issues will be addressed. Not involving the right people can lead you to a false conclusion.

Q: How do you determine whether a question is appropriate or not?

A: Appropriate questions will provide answers that lead to the right decision. A focus that is too narrow will not lead to a correct assessment or conclusion. Use the objective for the assessment as a guide to developing questions.

Q: Which aspects of needs assessment do you need to work on? How will you do that?

A: Answers will vary with each participant.

NEEDS ASSESSMENT APPLICATION CASE STUDY 56

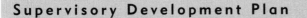

Supervisory Development Plan

Directions: Table 13.1 lists data collected from a survey of twelve assembly-line supervisors and 100 assembly-line workers. The survey asked respondents to identify the top three choices for suggested one-day workshops for supervisors. Additionally, supervisors were also asked to identify suggested one-day workshops for their peers. The surveys were tabulated and the top three choices for each group and each category are listed below along with narrative comments from the assembly-line workers. Review the data and recommend four one-day workshops. Keep in mind that these supervisors have never attended any type of supervisory training. Provide a rationale for your choices and suggest an appropriate sequence for presenting the four workshops.

Comments from Assembly-Line Workers

"It would really help my boss to listen before he climbs all over my case. I'd like some help from him—instead of him always trying to write someone up. He thinks he's a real tough guy."

"I've seen an improvement in communication in the last month. That's the key to everything. We need more of that."

"Supervisors need to get more done through the foreman. Give each foreman an area to be responsible for instead of trying to do everything himself. This would free up your supervisors to make decisions, effect meaningful planning, and be more knowledgeable about all areas of the line."

"Supervisors need to have a more positive attitude. They are kind of suspicious, most of the time. A little praise for a job well done would be appreciated."

"In the past my supervisor has had a double standard. He's also not very good at listening."

"The supervisors are under constant and excessive pressure and lack understanding from upper management about what really goes on down here."

"My supervisor lacks confidence. He changes his mind too easily."

"Maybe asking questions before jumping to conclusions about what has and has not been done, and who did it."

"More positive attitude toward labor relations."

"Act on employee's suggestions. Delegating more authority to us would create more harmony."

Table13.1. Survey Results.

Supervisors Say "I Need . . ."	*Other Supervisors Need . . .*	*Workers Say Supervisors Need . . .*
Personal Skills	**Personal Skills**	**Personal Skills**
Time Management	Time Management	Problem Solving and Decision Making
Problem Solving and Decision Making	Active Listening	Active Listening
Stress Management	Problem Solving and Decision Making	Time Management
Interpersonal Skills	**Interpersonal Skills**	**Interpersonal Skills**
Coaching/Counseling	Team Building	Team Building
Motivation	Motivation	Effective Communication
Team Building	Coaching/Counseling	Motivation
Effective Communication		Conflict Management
Supervisory Skills	**Supervisory Skills**	**Supervisory Skills**
Leadership Styles	Goal Setting	Leadership Styles
Training Subordinates	Leadership Styles	Labor Relations
Goal Setting	Training Subordinates	Delegation

What four workshops do you recommend for these supervisors? List them in a suggested sequence.

Facilitator Notes for Case Study 56

LEARNING OBJECTIVE: Given a case study, the participants will interpret needs assessment data, select four one-day workshops as part of a "Supervisory Development Plan," and provide a rationale for the selection of four one-day workshops for assembly-line supervisors.

Possible Case Answers

Four workshops recommended by the actual management team for this organization are

1. Leadership (to include elements of directing, coaching, and delegation)
2. Effective Communication (to include elements of active listening)
3. Problem Solving and Decision Making
4. Motivation and Discipline

The rationale for these choices is to look at workshops recommended in all three columns. Others often can more easily and more accurately recommend training needs. Individuals sometime find it difficult to distinguish between personal needs and wants. For that reason, greater weight is given to the second and third column in the survey data.

Sometimes each group named the same issue differently. In the supervisory skills lists, the supervisors name "Training Subordinates" as a popular choice for themselves and their peers. The workers are requesting training in "Delegation." In this organization, often supervisors did not delegate to subordinates because they were untrained. They explained, "If they were better trained, I would delegate more jobs to them."

After discussing "Time Management" and "Stress Management," the managers agreed that supervisors are not personally disorganized and are working "lots of overtime" because of an unusual increase in orders. This issue will go away on its own in two months. Also, by improving the supervisors' skills in leadership, communication, and problem solving and decision making, some of the symptoms of stress and time management would diminish.

Team Building was not recommended since these groups were barely communicating. This topic was too sophisticated for those who have never worked on leadership and communication skills.

The four workshops are listed in the original sequence. At the end of the second workshop, supervisors were asked to list the types of problems they face on a daily basis. Almost all problems they listed were related to disciplining employees. Therefore, "Motivation and Discipline" was presented as the third workshop and "Problem Solving and Decision Making" was presented as the fourth workshop.

Facilitator Processing Questions and Potential Answers

Q: What made it easy or difficult to select the four workshops from the survey data?

A: Seeing data displayed in a table makes it easier to identify workshops selected by more than one group. It is not easy to extract general information by reading through narrative comments.

Q: When analyzing survey data, what factors helped you select a specific course as a priority?

A: Courses were selected as a priority if more than one group selected a course or if the topic was similar to a topic in another column, even if it has a different title.

Q: How did you sequence the four topics?

A: Rationales may vary with individuals. Encourage participants to explain their rationale.

Q: What is significant about this type of data collection?

A: The information derived through this type of data collection needs to be discussed by all the stakeholders in order to produce the best and most effective training plan. Different stakeholders usually have different conclusions about how to interpret the same data.

NEEDS ASSESSMENT SERIAL CASE STUDY 57

Just-in-Time Training

Directions: Read the case study, and identify the purpose of conducting a needs assessment, the people to involve in the needs assessment, the type of information you will collect, how you will collect the information, and how you will use the information to develop a suggestion to report to the Branch Manager.

The Branch Manager says that Paul Gomez, a new teller, "must have been sleeping part of the time during Teller Training." He says, "We're going to lose a lot of money on this one!" He wants you to come out to the branch and observe the many mistakes he is making and work with him so he is as capable as the other new tellers that were in a recent Teller School class you conducted.

You remember Paul as a slow, methodical learner who seemed to learn best by doing a task several times. Although you found it necessary to explain and demonstrate a process more than once, when he finished the three-week Teller School, he demonstrated all of the paying and receiving functions correctly.

Paul's native language is Spanish and he is an immigrant from Guatemala. Occasionally, he seemed to be thinking a process through in his native language and often talked to himself in Spanish when methodically performing the steps in a process. Surely he could not have forgotten what he learned just a short time ago. You remember this class of new tellers required additional practice time to learn new skills, so the final two days of training were rushed to get all the content covered. Is retraining or feedback and coaching the answer?

The Manager of the Teller School would prefer you use your time co-facilitating the next session of Teller School that will begin in a week. She believes, "The Branch Managers and Operations Supervisors sometimes get lazy and don't want to do the follow-up supervision and coaching that is required for new employees."

1. What is the purpose of conducting a needs assessment?
2. What people will you involve in the needs assessment?

3. What type of information will you collect?
4. How you will collect the information?
5. How you will use the information to develop a suggestion to report to the Branch Manager?

Needs Assessment Serial Case Study 57

LEARNING OBJECTIVE: Given a case study, the learner will practice correctly completing all phases of a needs assessment.

Possible Case Answers

1. The purpose of conducting a needs assessment is to identify what will help the new teller perform to the Branch Manager's expectations.
2. People you will involve in the needs assessment include:
   - Paul Gomez, the new teller
   - The Branch Manager
   - Paul's Operations Supervisor
   - The Manager of the Teller School
   - Other trainers who taught the three-week school
3. The type of information will you collect includes:
   - The results of performance tests for Paul conducted during Teller School.
   - What processes Paul cannot complete correctly.
   - The type of follow-up expected of Management at the Branch.
   - The expectations of the Manager of the Teller School for appropriate follow-up done by either Teller School Trainers and/or Branch Management.
   - Whether the methods used to teach processes during training are appropriate for different learning styles and the target population now being hired by the Bank.
   - The types of job aids provided to new employees to remind them of all the steps in processes.
   - The reasons for possible differences in training results for Paul and the other teller trainees in the same school class.

4. How you will collect the information?
    - Discussions
    - Interviews
    - Observations
    - Review test results
5. How you will use the information to develop a suggestion to report to the Branch Manager?
    - Compile written and anecdotal information.
    - Suggest a meeting with the Manager of the Teller School at the Branch and include the Branch Manager and the Operations Supervisor.

Facilitator Processing Questions and Potential Answers

Q: What are all the phases of a complete needs assessment?

A: The phases of a needs assessment include:

- Establishing the objective
- Gain agreement for the objective with your manager
- Include relevant parties
- Gain agreement on developing relevant types of information and how information will be collected
- Collect information that is not disruptive to the work of the organization
- Interpret information
- Report back and discuss information with those who asked for the assessment
- Make recommendations or reach decisions using a process that is in keeping with the organization's norms

Q: Which parts seem easy or difficult for you to complete?

A: Answers will vary with each participant.

Q: Which parts need further development?

A: Answers will vary with each participant.

Q: What is the key to completing a needs assessment successfully?

A: The key elements to completing a needs assessment successfully are an agreed-upon objective, collecting relevant information, and using a decision-making process that is appropriate for the organization's norms.

14

New Employee Orientation

THIS CHAPTER contains five types of case studies that teach various lessons about how to design and conduct a new employee orientation. Managers, supervisors, and trainers who design and conduct new employee orientation can use these case studies to meet their needs. Case studies in this chapter might be used in "leadership, supervisor, management" or "new employee orientation" classes.

See the Introduction to Part 2 on pages 63–64 for suggestions on how to select and customize the case studies in this chapter.

NEW EMPLOYEE ORIENTATION IDENTIFICATION CASE STUDY 58

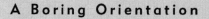

A Boring Orientation

Directions: What works well in this orientation, and what needs to be improved?

You are in the process of revising the organization's New Employee Orientation program. To learn more about the existing new employee orientation, you sit through one of the typical monthly new employee meetings and interview several supervisors of new employees and employees who have been with the company for less than six months. You learn the following about the orientation meeting:

- Most employees are treated politely.
- Most employees ask only a few questions.
- The format of orientation repeats itself: each guest speaker has fifteen minutes to explain a policy, procedure, or department function.
- Handout material and copies of slides provided by some speakers duplicate verbal information almost word-for-word.
- There is too much information on the slides and it is difficult to read them from even the middle to rear of the room.
- The length of the facility tour often is shortened because speakers do not stay within their time limit.
- The benefits presentation was an endless stream of paperwork. Trying to compare one health care plan to another was difficult by just reading each company's literature.
- Employees said the introduction to telephone skills training and the video on the company's history were the best parts of the orientation.

What works well in this orientation and what needs to be improved?

Facilitator Notes for Case Study 58

LEARNING OBJECTIVE: Given a case study, the learner will identify the elements of a successful new employee orientation.

Possible Case Answers

What works well?

- Most employees are treated politely.
- Employees said the introduction to telephone skills training and the video on the company's history were the best parts of the orientation.

What needs to be improved?

- Most employees ask only a few questions.
- The format of orientation repeats itself: each guest speaker has fifteen minutes to explain a policy, procedure, or department function.
- Handout material and copies of slides provided by some speakers duplicate verbal information almost word-for-word.
- There is too much information on the slides and it is difficult to read them from even the middle to rear of the room.
- The length of the facility tour often is shortened because speakers do not stay within their time limit.
- The benefits presentation was an endless stream of paperwork. Trying to compare one health care plan to another was difficult by just reading each company's literature.

Facilitator Processing Questions and Potential Answers

Q: What are the successful elements of any new employee orientation process?

A: These are successful elements as demonstrated in either a positive or negative way in the case study:

- Use a variety of mediums (video, slides, guest speakers, etc.).
- Use a variety of methods (skills training, presentations to learn essential information, presentation of corporate culture).
- People are treated politely and something positive is done to confirm employees have made a right decision by joining the organization.
- Use adult learning methods rather than read to people from slides or handout materials, allow them to read for themselves.
- Support guest speakers with specific objectives, handouts, and visual aids and keep within a time limit. Transfer some long-winded speakers to video presentations.
- Move the facilities tour earlier in the day. After lunch is a great time to keep the pace alive with a tour.
- Create a few typical questions or have new employees write questions or expectations as a part of a climate setting activity at the beginning of the session. Post answers to frequently asked questions on the organization's Intranet.
- Present complex information in an easy-to-read format, such as a table to compare the benefits of different health plans.
- Make new employee orientation a process that presents information over a period of time (one to three months) and tells employees what they need, closest to the time information is needed.

Q: What can be done in your organization to improve new employee orientation?

A: Answers will vary with each participant.

Q: If you could only work on one way to improve your new employee orientation, what is your priority?

A: Answers will vary with each participant.

NEW EMPLOYEE ORIENTATION PROBLEM SOLVING CASE STUDY 59

Get Supervisors Involved

Directions: Review the twelve critical elements that follow from Successful New Employee Orientation, *(2nd edition, Pfeiffer, 2001) by Jean Barbazette. As you read this case study, keep the twelve elements in mind and identify issues that need to be addressed if new employee orientation is to be successful in this organization.*

1. All effective programs view orientation as an ongoing process, not just a one-day program.
2. Because orientation is an ongoing process, information is given to the new employee closest to the time it is needed.
3. The benefits of orientation are clear and visible to both the new employee and the organization.
4. Successful orientation programs shared their "corporate culture" (philosophy, how to get along, how business is done, etc.).
5. The employee's first day is truly welcoming and helps the employee feel useful and productive.
6. The supervisor's role in New Employee Orientation (NEO) is clear and well executed with human resources department's or function's assistance.
7. Orientation objectives in successful organizations are measurable and focus on specific knowledge, skill acquisition, and influencing attitudes.
8. Adult learning concepts are known and used to guide orientation.
9. Successful guest speakers are well prepared, present only essential information with specific objectives, and use good presentation techniques.
10. Audiovisual components of successful NEO programs provide emphasis to the program and provide a positive message.

11. The NEO process is evaluated by participants, supervisors, and the human resources department or function from bottom-line results.
12. Successful NEO programs provide information to the employee's family.

You are a Human Resources Assistant and have been given an assignment to develop a New Employee Orientation program for all employees. Most new employees hired to work at the grocery warehouse are assigned to the night shift between 11:00 PM and 8:00 AM. This is the slowest of the three shifts. New employees have the opportunity to receive extensive procedures and safety training when normal activity is minimal. Union representatives are also allowed three hours of meeting time with new employees during the first week of employment for their part of orientation.

There has also been lots of turnover on night shift. During exit interviews, it is learned that those who don't stay long feel humiliated by public reprimands from supervisors and also feel cheated by the lack of training for the tasks they are expected to do.

When you have discussed the idea of a more comprehensive new employee orientation with the night supervisor, he chastises the Human Resources Department for hiring a bunch of kids who "can't take it like I did when I was coming up." And, he asks, "Why don't you hire experienced people who don't need training or orientation?"

The warehouse has no formal orientation. Your current assignment is to develop a New Employee Orientation that will be conducted jointly by supervisors and Human Resources. What are the issues to address if orientation is to be successful?

Facilitator Notes for Case Study 59

LEARNING OBJECTIVE: Given a case study, the learner will identify problems that prevent a new employee orientation from being successful and suggest steps to resolve these problems.

Possible Case Answers

The issues to address if orientation is to be successful include:

- The night shift supervisor has an unrealistic picture of today's labor pool and new employees require skills training to do the jobs to the company's expectation and avoid accidents.
- Required skills and safety training are not completed during the tenure of new employees on the night shift.
- The night shift supervisor publicly reprimands new employees and apparently expects new employees to endure this type of treatment.
- If both supervisors and Human Resources personnel will conduct the new employee orientation, no mutual respect or support seems to exist.

Suggestions to resolve these problems might include:

- Encouraging the night supervisor to change his behavior, or replace him with another supervisor who uses different methods to train and encourage new employees.
- Review the objectives, content, and methods of the required skills and safety training and identify how it could be improved.
- Discuss orientation issues with supervisors and identify the benefits for them of a well-oriented new employee. Sort tasks to be completed by each group as a part of new employee orientation.

Facilitator Processing Questions and Potential Answers

Q: What types of resources and support are needed for a successful new employee orientation?

A: The types of resources and support needed for a successful new employee orientation include:

- Support from upper management who believes in the benefits of new employee orientation (retention, reduction of accidents, etc.).
- Time for supervisors and Human Resources personnel to develop and present new employee orientation.
- Sufficient budget for equipment and materials to develop and present orientation.
- Supervisory support to allow new employees the time to attend orientation sessions.
- Availability of information in a variety of media and formats for the new employee.
- Use of a "buddy" to assist the new employee and involvement of other employees to coach, mentor, and develop new employees.
- Partnership among all stakeholders who need to be involved in the program.

Q: What aspect of your new employee orientation is problematic?

A: Answers will vary with each participant.

Q: How can you address those problems?

A: Answers will vary with each participant.

NEW EMPLOYEE ORIENTATION PRACTICE CASE STUDY 60

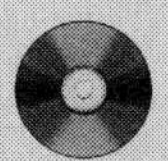

Improvement Needed

Directions: As you read the case study, think of suggestions to improve the content and delivery of this orientation.

Jeremy feels a bit badly about his newly hired employees, but there is just so much work to be done! Typically he spends the first hour or so with the new person telling him everything he can think of about the store. Then he sits him down to read the product and operating manuals while he gets back to work. Reading about company products and procedures takes most of the new employee's time during the first day. Sometime during the first day Jeremy usually asks his assistant to give the new hire a store tour and show him where he can put his personal stuff. Then he assigns the new person to dust and organize stock—this unconsciously helps the person become familiar with the variety of items in the store.

If you were to redesign this new employee orientation, what can you suggest to improve content and delivery of this orientation?

Facilitator Notes for Case Study 60

LEARNING OBJECTIVE: Given a case study, the learner will identify how to improve the content and delivery of a new employee orientation.

Possible Case Answers

Content improvement:

- The current content is limited to what Jeremy can think of about the store and the product and operating manuals.
- Information about the "bigger picture" would help the new employees recognize the importance of their roles and responsibilities in fulfilling the mission and vision of the organization.
- Anticipating and providing answers to frequently asked questions could be helpful to new employees.
- Use marketing and advertising materials to show the new employee how the company and its products are portrayed.

Delivery improvement:

- A written agenda or list of topics to cover for the first day and first week would help Jeremy provide a consistent delivery.
- Provide some training in stock inventory and management processes prior to giving a new employee responsibility to "dust and organize." Help the employee consciously become familiar with the variety of items by sharing that objective and elevating the importance of what could be seen as a mundane task.
- Provide an alternative to only reading about products and operating procedures.
- Involve the new employee in a variety of knowledge and skill building activities during the first days of orientation. Provide information about the company culture, such as how to fit in, get work done, and identify norms.

- Ask the new employees to complete some self-discovery assignments (interview other employees or customers, do Internet searches about competing products, complete a scavenger hunt, go on a self-guided tour, etc.) and report back to you or a "buddy" to discuss what they have learned.

Facilitator Processing Questions and Potential Answers

Q: What redesign steps are needed to improve a new employee orientation?

A: Redesign steps follow most instructional systems design (ISD) processes and include:

- Assess what the existing program does well and identify areas for improvement.
- Assess and plan to gather information from the target population, identify benefits for the new employee and the organization.
- Build a partnership with stakeholders so they will support and participate appropriately in an orientation.
- Write objectives for an orientation.
- Develop content to include that meets the objectives and delivers the benefits of an orientation.
- Create interactive adult learning methods that encourage new employees to complete an orientation.
- Evaluate the orientation for the new employee's reaction, learning, use of information, and bottom-line results.

Q: What makes it easy or difficult to redesign a new employee orientation?

A: It is easy to redesign an orientation if you have the commitment of stakeholders and the resources to complete the job. It is difficult to complete a redesign without commitment and resources. Knowledge of successful orientation programs to use as a model are helpful as well as experience and expertise in designing this type of program.

Q: What do you need to do to make the task of designing or redesigning your organization's new employee orientation?

A: Answers will vary with each participant.

NEW EMPLOYEE ORIENTATION APPLICATION CASE STUDY 61

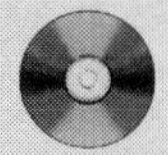

Commitment Is Critical

Directions: As you read the case study, identify how you can gain greater commitment from supervisors to allow their employees to attend the entire new employee orientation process.

You work in an organization that conducts New Employee Orientation during the first week of employment through a series of meetings. The first two to three hours of the first day are for essential paperwork and a tour. Human Resources Department conducts this meeting. The rest of the first day is spent in the employee's new department.

New employees are "invited" back to a second information session at the end of the first week. The agenda for the second session includes:

- Company history
- How to fit in and be successful
- Organization chart and how departments work together
- Company products and services
- Overview of training programs available
- Emergency and security procedures
- Conflict of interest and confidentiality

Many supervisors think the meeting is a waste of productive time, especially when the department is short-handed. A few supervisors are openly hostile and brag about not allowing their employees to attend this "frivolous" meeting. Their new people ought to be able to pick this stuff up by reading a handbook. You consider this information critical to the success of each new employee. How can you gain support from the supervisors for the follow-up meeting?

Facilitator Notes for Case Study 61

LEARNING OBJECTIVE: Given a case study, the learner will apply what you know about gaining commitment from stakeholders and make suggestions to improve the results of new employee orientation.

Possible Case Answers

Support from supervisors for the follow-up meeting can be increased by:

- Having managers hold supervisors accountable for new employees' attendance at the follow-up meeting.
- Having supervisors identify the benefits of having new employees attend the follow-up meeting.
- Having supervisors identify the cost of new employees violating emergency and security procedures.
- Asking the supervisors how they would prefer to have new employees effectively handle topics covered at the follow-up meeting besides reading a handbook.

Facilitator Processing Questions and Potential Answers

Q: What makes it easy or difficult to gain commitment from supervisors?

A: It is easier to gain commitment from supervisors when the benefits of attending orientation are known and aligned with what the supervisors value. Commitment is less likely when benefits are unknown and program values are not aligned with what supervisors value.

Q: How have you gained or can you gain commitment from supervisors in your organization to a new employee orientation process?

A: Answers will vary with each participant.

Q: Which of the suggestions discussed here will help gain commitment for new employee orientation in your organization?

A: Answers will vary with each participant.

NEW EMPLOYEE ORIENTATION SERIAL CASE STUDY 62

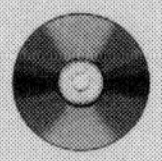

There's Got to Be a Better Way

Directions: Using the first case study in this chapter, address these issues:

- *What is being done well and what needs improvement?*
- *What problems exist in the existing program?*
- *What are your suggestions to overcome these problems?*
- *How will you redesign the orientation program to include the twelve critical elements to make new employee orientation successful?*
- *How will you gain commitment for the new orientation process from all stakeholders?*

Use case study answers and facilitator processing questions provided with each case in this chapter.

15

Supervision

THIS CHAPTER contains five types of case studies that teach various lessons about how to supervise employees in a work situation. New and experienced managers, supervisors, and those who want to become supervisors can benefit from these case studies. Case studies in this chapter might be used in "leadership, supervision or management" classes.

See the Introduction to Part 2 on pages 63–64 for suggestions on how to select and customize the case studies in this chapter.

SUPERVISION IDENTIFICATION CASE STUDY 63

Sue Weldon, New Supervisor

Directions: As you read the case study,

- *Underline the things you think Sue is doing correctly.*
- *Bracket [ ] the things you think Sue is doing incorrectly.*
- *Decide if you would like Sue to work for you or if you would like to work for Sue.*

Sue Weldon is a highly regarded charge nurse and a bit of a perfectionist. She was promoted into a supervisory position six months ago because she is one of the best surgical staff nurses at the Medical Center.

Sue is a methodical planner and closely supervises the unit that helps patients recover from surgery. Sue says, "It's my job to get employees to provide the best patient care possible and do that in the most cost-effective manner possible. If anyone is doing something wrong, I tell him or her exactly what to do. I have learned to size up a problem quickly. I'm concerned about quality care for our patients. I have learned to get to the heart of the matter. My biggest problem is getting the rest of the staff to focus on care delivery. There's so much emphasis on cost containment. They must remember we're here to help patients recover from surgery and be well enough by the time they are discharged."

Upper management respects Sue for her good judgment. Sue tends to think through an issue and then make all of the decisions herself. Sue believes she is pretty good at selling her decisions to her staff. A major concern is losing authority over her staff, so she is loathe to admit making a mistake. When an employee does an excellent job, Sue is quick to compliment them. She is often concerned about solving problems, and when she finds the guilty party, her facts are listed in rapid fire order and her criticism can be sharp, often in front of others.

Employees complain Sue seldom asks their opinions on anything. They feel neglected and ignored.

The Unit rarely fails to meet its targets and always gets high marks on patient satisfaction surveys. To make sure productivity and satisfaction levels remain high, Sue frequently stays beyond the end of her shift to finish a job and complete planning tasks. Medical Center administration is pleased with Sue's Unit, but the Vice President of Nursing is concerned that Sue is working excessive overtime and it could affect her health.

Facilitator Notes for Case Study 63

LEARNING OBJECTIVE: Given a case study, the supervisor will identify four pitfalls of new supervisors and strategies to overcome each pitfall.

Possible Case Answers

What is Sue doing correctly?

- She was an excellent Medical/Surgical Staff Nurse.
- She is a careful planner.
- She is concerned about quality care for patients.
- She can size up a problem quickly.
- She is known for her good judgment.
- She compliments employees when they do an outstanding job.
- Sue's department gets the work out on time and in good shape.

What is Sue doing incorrectly?

- She is a perfectionist.
- She exercises close, detailed supervision over her subordinates.
- She almost always tells her subordinates exactly what to do.
- She makes all the decisions herself.
- She seldom admits making an error.
- She publicly criticizes employees who make mistakes.
- She rarely asks employees for their opinions.
- She is stretching herself too thin by staying late to finish a job or polish up on a few things.

Facilitator Processing Questions and Potential Answers

Q: What are the behaviors of an effective supervisor?

A: Effective supervisors:

- Set goals and objectives with employees.
- Share expectations and train subordinates to meet those expectations.
- Different techniques that appropriately meet a goal or objective should not be discounted.
- Include subordinates in planning, ask for and implement suggestions from employees.
- Praise in public and criticize in private.
- Make a learning opportunity out of a mistake.
- Manage time realistically by developing subordinates and delegating responsibly.

Q: What circumstances make it easy or difficult for a new supervisor to be effective with subordinates?

A: Four pitfalls often encountered by new supervisors include:

- Inappropriate priorities: trying to accomplish the work by doing too much yourself, instead of delegating work that others can complete.
- Not spending enough time in planning, including soliciting and using the ideas of subordinates.
- Wanting to be liked by subordinates as friends versus gaining respect by leading effectively.
- Exercising too little or too much control over the work of others.

Q: How can a new supervisor overcome some of these pitfalls when supervising others?

A: To overcome the four pitfalls, try:

- Focus on accomplishments, not just keeping busy. Learn how to delegate tasks and responsibility for the results.
- Ask subordinates for suggestions as part of the planning process. Create a workable plan, share your expectations and train subordinates in the skills to accomplish the results. Give feedback and coach as appropriate.
- Find a coach or mentor outside your work group. Do not complain about work problems to subordinates in a social setting. Make new friends. Be friendly, genuine, and sincere.
- Assess whether an employee can do a job, share your expectations and deadlines, and provide appropriate tools and supplies along with encouragement. The best feedback comes from the work itself. Find ways to check on results without being overbearing and directly supervising others.

Q: What characteristics are important for you to develop? How will you do that?

A: Answers will vary with each participant.

SUPERVISION PROBLEM SOLVING CASE STUDY 64

That's My Job

Directions: As you read the case study, identify the problems facing the new supervisor. What suggestions can you offer the supervisor to make a successful transition into this new position?

You have just been hired as the Director of Housekeeping by a major hotel chain at one of its premier 1,000-room big city properties. You have been working your way up the career ladder in this organization for fifteen years by working for the same chain and taking promotions or transfers to larger properties when openings occur. You are new to this property and new to this city. Your experience as a Director of Housekeeping is at a smaller property.

You will have five supervisors reporting to you: three are day supervisors, one is a night supervisor, and one supervises the laundry. The hotel has been slow in making the transition to a permanent Director of Housekeeping, since the former Director died unexpectedly in an automobile accident three months ago. During the last three months Yolanda Gomez, the senior day supervisor, has been the Interim Director of Housekeeping. Yolanda was surprised the hotel went outside the property for a new Director rather than give her the permanent appointment. She feels you are taking "her" job.

Yolanda clearly does not have the education, skill, or preparation to do the demanding tasks of a Director. Although she is well liked by the Housekeeping staff, she lacks the planning and budgeting skills of a director.

Bill is the most experienced and talented lead person of the Housekeeping staff. He temporarily filled Yolanda's supervisory position while the hotel looked for a permanent Director. Bill is young and ambitious and has two years to finish his college degree in Hospitality Management. While he benefits from the hotel's generous tuition reimbursement program, he does not want to give up the status and experience he gained from the temporary supervisory position. On your first day of work, he threatens to quit if he has to go back to a lead role.

Because of the circumstances of the prior Director's death and the uncertainty that developed during the length of time taken to fill that position, morale has been low. Management has given you three weeks to submit next year's staffing plan and budget.

1. What are the problems you face as the new Director of Housekeeping?
2. What are your suggestions to solve these problems?

Facilitator Notes for Case Study 64

LEARNING OBJECTIVE: Given a case study, the supervisor will identify the problems facing this new supervisor and make appropriate suggestions for handling these problems.

Possible Case Answers

1. What are the problems you face as the new Director of Housekeeping?
   - The senior supervisor resents you taking "her" job.
   - The hotel took three months to fill the Director position and morale deteriorated during that time.
   - Bill, the interim supervisor, is threatening to quit.
   - You need to put together a staffing plan and budget in the next three weeks while you are getting to know the staff and how supervisors do their jobs at this hotel.
2. What are your suggestions to solve these problems?
   - Discuss management's understanding with Yolanda about her interim responsibilities and any promises made to her about permanent placement as the Director.
   - Discuss Yolanda's career options and clarify your expectations of her as the senior supervisor.
   - Work on getting to know all of the supervisors and staff, and identify what incentives would improve morale for this group.
   - Discuss long-term career options and benefits with Bill. If he is too impatient, perhaps he would be better off somewhere else. Discuss his options with upper management and the possibility of having him enter the management intern program.

- Study the current staffing plan and budgets. Review the hotel's plans for the next year, and identify how those plans will impact your department during the coming year.

Facilitator Processing Questions and Potential Answers

Q: What makes it easy or difficult to become the new supervisor or manager of an existing work group?

A: New supervisors are not aware of past history with the work group. Finding out as much as possible about the work group can help make the transition smoother. It is sometimes difficult for a supervisor to fit into an existing work group. To some extent, the supervisor needs to clarify his or her expectations and ask the group to change how they accomplish their work to be more effective. Be careful about making too many changes before observing what is working well from the past supervisor.

Q: How do you deal with employees who feel they are being treated unfairly?

A: Hear out the employees and document their side of the complaint. Clarify your expectations and ask what can be done, given the circumstances, to make the "wronged" employee feel that she or he is being treated fairly.

Q: What do you need to do to work more effectively as a new supervisor?

A: Answers will vary with each participant.

SUPERVISION PRACTICE CASE STUDY 65

Giving Orders

Directions: Read the following situation. Answer the five questions to prepare for a discussion with others.

Your manager has asked you to arrange the conference room for an orientation to your company of a group of very important visitors. There will be about 20 people attending the meeting and you want to make a good impression. Because several offices have been moved recently, the conference room has been used to store boxes. Making such arrangements is not part of your duties, but no one else is available at the moment.

You have asked two people to help you set up the room. One of them, Mary, is with you. She is your new support person. Jim, a custodian, has not shown up yet. The meeting will take place in two hours. In addition to some heavy cartons, the room is overcrowded with chairs and is dusty. You envision seating the visitors around the conference table. A slide presentation will be shown on the front wall; no screen is available.

1. You have an idea of how you want to arrange the room. Write down exactly what you would say to Mary in one sentence.
2. You decide to first clear the area for the projector. You want Mary to help you move some heavy cartons. What do you say to Mary?
3. After you have been dusting chairs for 20 minutes, Jim shows up. Working has been difficult because the room is overcrowded with cartons. What do you say to Jim?
4. Jim is trying to lift a heavy carton by himself, instead of asking for help or using a hand truck (which is downstairs). You are concerned Jim will hurt his back. What do you say?

5. Finally the room looks as it should. You sit down in one of the chairs to rest a bit, and notice that the wall directly opposite the projector has an electrical box in the center of it. It will be impossible to show the presentation on that wall. The table will have to be moved down and the projector moved to the other end of the room. What do you say to Jim and Mary?

Facilitator Notes for Case Study 65

LEARNING OBJECTIVE: Given a case study, practice appropriately giving orders to others to get the results you need. Appropriate means the right amount of directions by suggesting, requesting, instructing, or commanding.

Possible Case Answers

1. "My manager needs this room to conduct a meeting for twenty people. We need to clear out the boxes and clean up the conference room. There will also be a slide presentation."
2. "Mary, if both of us work together, we might be able to slide some of these bigger boxes out of the way. Can you do that without hurting yourself?"
3. "Jim, I'm glad you're here. We need your help to clear these boxes out of the conference room for a meeting."
4. "Jim, I don't want you to hurt your back. Stop moving the cartons and get the hand truck from downstairs."
5. "We have a problem. I didn't see that electrical box in the center of the wall. How else can the manager show a presentation in this room?"

Facilitator Processing Questions and Potential Answers

Q: What made it easy or difficult to find the right words to give orders to a new support person?

A: If you don't know the people you are directing, it may be difficult to use the right amount of direction. You need to decide how to frame your direction by making it a suggestion, request, instruction, or order.

Q: How is giving directions different when the person receiving your direction doesn't report to you?

A: You may not be aware of this person's skill level or how he will react to your direction. The idea is to give the appropriate amount of direction without being too demanding.

Q: What are characteristics of a supervisor who appropriately directs the work of subordinates?

A: The supervisor who appropriately directs the work of subordinates will

- Identify problems
- Set goals and define roles
- Develop plans to solve problems
- Decide what, how, when, and with whom
- Give specific directions
- Use mostly one-way communication
- Maintain responsibility for problem solving and decision making
- Tell solutions and decisions

Q: What did you learn about giving directions from this exercise?

A: Answers will vary with each participant.

SUPERVISION APPLICATION CASE STUDY 66

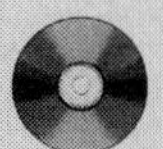

How to Support Employees

Directions: If you were this supervisor, how would you appropriately support your employees? What specific behaviors would be appropriate for you to support and coach these employees? Supporting behavior is defined as a supervisor and the employees share problem solving and decision making with the key roles of the supervisor being listening and facilitating.

Your store has been asked by the owner of the chain of stores to develop and evaluate a new computer inventory system on a pilot basis. This would mean that the new system would be worked in a redundant (parallel) manner with the present system. To do this will make your employees' work demanding for at least the next two months. One of the key reasons your store has been approached to accomplish this job is because of your high level of confidence in them, which you have often expressed to the owner.

If your store succeeds, there will probably be significant rewards for your efforts. There is also a fairly high risk of failure, which, while not leading to any penalties, would mean far less in rewards. You and your employees have enjoyed an excellent relationship with mutual trust and respect existing among all of you. You suspect that this might be tested somewhat because of the demands of running two systems in parallel. However, you strongly feel that the possible benefits outweigh the risks and you want to develop the new system. Your answer is due to the owner by the end of the month.

What specific behaviors would be appropriate for you to support and coach these employees?

Facilitator Notes for Case Study 66

LEARNING OBJECTIVE: Given a case study, the learner will apply appropriate supporting behaviors as a supervisor.

Possible Case Answers

Supportive behaviors include:

- Discussing the objectives of the inventory pilot with your employees.
- Discussing the benefits and risks of participating in the pilot.
- Discuss how the challenges presented by the pilot may hurt the group and ask the employees for their ideas to meet the challenges.
- Reveal how much input you are seeking to make this decision.

Facilitator Processing Questions and Potential Answers

Q: What factors ought to be in place for a supervisor to select supportive behavior when trying to make this type of decision?

A: Factors that ought to be in place include:

- An informed group of workers who have the knowledge, skill, and maturity to consider information and arrive at a reasoned decision.
- Enough time to hold the discussions this style of supervision requires.
- The risks and rewards will be shared equally for the group.
- The group has the confidence of the supervisor and other team members.

Q: What are supporting behaviors that you favor with your work team?

A: Answers will vary with each participant.

Q: What are supporting behaviors you want to develop?

A: Answers will vary with each participant.

Q: How will you develop your work team so you can involve them in decision making appropriately when supportive behavior would make sense?

A: Answers will vary with each participant.

SUPERVISION SERIAL CASE STUDY 67

One Step from Retirement

Directions: As you read this case study, identify the behaviors of the new supervisor that might be causing difficulty. What are the pitfalls and how could this supervisor overcome these barriers to better performance? What directive and supportive behaviors would be appropriate for the supervisor to use with this team?

A few weeks ago, the department manager told Gwen, the supervisor, that she would accept Stanley, an older, long-time employee into your work group. Stanley has been minimally effective in his other work assignments and for reasons unclear to Gwen; he cannot be fired or reassigned to another region.

There have been rumors Gwen has yet to investigate about Stanley not completing simple job assignments. She feels sorry for Stanley, but now the rest of the group has come to Gwen to protest accepting Stanley into the group. They are very specific in saying that Stanley is not contributing and others have to do part of his work to accomplish team goals. A few of the team members are rather vocal about a work slowdown if something is not done to change the situation.

Gwen has usually been effective at convincing the team to do what she thinks is correct and she feels she can be successful again, since the manager has given her permission to speak candidly to the team about the reason Stanley has joined the work group.

1. Identify the behaviors of the new supervisor that might be causing difficulty.
2. What are the pitfalls, and how could this supervisor overcome these barriers to better performance?
3. What directive and supportive behaviors would be appropriate for the supervisor to use with this team?

Facilitator Notes for Case Study 67

LEARNING OBJECTIVE: Given a case study, identify how the pitfalls of a new supervisor appear, identify the problems that result from not avoiding these pitfalls, and identify skills the new supervisor can develop to avoid these pitfalls in the future. Also identify appropriate directive and supportive behaviors that would be appropriate either now or in the future.

Possible Case Answers

1. Identify the behaviors of the new supervisor that might be causing difficulty.
    - Gwen has not investigated rumors about Stanley not completing simple job assignments.
    - Although Gwen has her manager's permission to speak candidly to the team about the reason Stanley has joined the group, she has let the situation deteriorate, rather than address it directly.
2. What are the pitfalls, and how could this supervisor overcome these barriers to better performance?
    - Gwen feels sorry for Stanley and has allowed the rest of her team to deteriorate.
    - She could overcome this problem and improve team performance by discussing the issue with Stanley and the rest of her team.
3. What directive and supportive behaviors would be appropriate for the supervisor to use with this team?
    - Gwen feeling sorry for Stanley will not help get the team functioning productively. Gwen needs to be more directive with Stanley, share the team's goals and objectives, and her expectations for at least minimal performance. There also needs to be some enforceable consequences if Stanley refuses to be a functioning member of the team.

- Gwen needs to be directive with the team and tell them work slowdowns will not work to change anything. She has her manager's permission to share the reasons Stanley has joined the work group. She can offer this information to the team and enlist their support to find ways to return the team to a productive unit. The more supportive Gwen is with the rest of the team, the easier it will be for them to follow her leadership.

Facilitator Processing Questions and Potential Answers

Q: What are obstacles you have faced in your role as a supervisor to adapting or changing your behavior to be either more directive or supportive?

A: Answers will vary with each participant.

Q: How have you overcome these barriers?

A: Answers will vary with each participant.

Q: What will you continue to do or not do in order to get your team to be as productive as possible?

A: Answers will vary with each participant.

BIBLIOGRAPHY

Barbazette, Jean. 2001. *Successful New Employee Orientation.* 2nd ed. San Francisco: Pfeiffer/Jossey Bass.

______. 2001. *The Trainer's Support Handbook.* New York: McGraw-Hill.

Bell, Chip. 1982. *Influencing.* Austin, TX: Learning Concepts.

Bower, Sharon A., and Bower, Gordon H. 1976. *Asserting Yourself.* Cambridge, MA: Persus Books.

Brinkerhoff, Roberto. 2003. The Successful Case Method. San Francisco, CA: Berrett-Koehler Publishing Inc.

Ertmer, Peggy A., and Quinn, James. 1998. *The ID Casebook: Case Studies in Instructional Design.* New York: Prentice Hall.

Gardenswartz, Lee, and Lowe, Anita. 1998. *Managing Diversity.* New York: McGraw-Hill.

Gibson, Joanna. 2002. *Perspectives: Case Studies for Readers and Writers.* Harlow, Essex, UK: Pearson Education.

Kaner, Sam. 1996. *Facilitator's Guide to Participatory Decision-Making.* Gabriola Island, BC Canada: New Society Publishers.

Lynn, Laurence E. 1999. *Teaching and Learning with Cases: A Guidebook.* New York: Chatham House Publishers.

Mager, Robert. 1984. 2nd ed. *Analyzing Performance Problems.* Atlanta: Center for Effective Leadership.

Naumes, William, and Naumes, Margaret J. 1999. *The Art and Craft of Case Writing.* Thousand Oaks, CA: Sage Publications.

INDEX

N

P

R

S

T

AUTHOR CONTACT INFORMATION

If you have a case study to contribute to future volumes of *Instant Case Studies,* see the submission guidelines at www.thetrainingclinic.com and contact the author:

Jean Barbazette, President
The Training Clinic
645 Seabreeze Drive
Seal Beach, CA 90740
jean@thetrainingclinic.com
www.thetrainingclinic.com

System Requirements

Windows PC

- 486 or Pentium processor-based personal computer
- Microsoft Windows 95 or Windows NT 3.51 or later
- Minimum RAM: 8MB for Windows 95 and NT
- Available space on hard disk: 8MB Windows 95 and NT
- 2X speed CD-ROM drive or faster

Macintosh

- Macintosh with a 68020 or higher processor or Power Macintosh
- Apple OS version 7.0 or later
- Minimum RAM: 12MB for Macintosh
- Available space on hard disk: 6MB Macintosh
- 2X speed CD-ROM drive or faster

NOTE: This CD requires Netscape 3.0 or MS Internet Explorer 3.0 or higher. You can download these products using the links on the CD-ROM Help Page.

Getting Started

Insert the CD-ROM into your drive. The CD-ROM will usually launch automatically. If it does not, click on the CD-ROM drive on your computer to launch. After you click to agree to the terms of the Copyright Page, the Home Page will appear.

Moving Around

Use the buttons at the left of each screen to move among the menu pages. To view a document listed on one of the menu pages, simply click on the name of the document. To quit a document at any time, click the box at the upper right-hand corner of the screen.

To quit the CD-ROM, you can click the Exit button or hit Alt-F4.

To Download Documents

Open the document you wish to download. Under the File pull-down menu, choose Save As. Save the document onto your hard drive with a different name. It is important to use a different name, otherwise the document may remain a read-only file.

You can also click on your CD drive in Windows Explorer and select a document to copy it to your hard drive and rename it.

In Case of Trouble

If you experience difficulty using this CD-ROM, please follow these steps:

1. Make sure your hardware and systems configurations conform to the systems requirements noted under "Systems Requirements."

2. Review the installation procedure for your type of hardware and operating system. It is possible to reinstall the software if necessary.
3. Have a question, comment, or suggestion? Contact us! We value your feedback, and we want to hear from you.

For questions about this or other Pfeiffer products, you may contact us by:

E-mail: customer@wiley.com
Mail: Customer Care Wiley/Pfeiffer
10475 Crosspoint Blvd.
Indianapolis, IN 46256
Phone: (U.S.) 800–274–4434 (Outside the U.S. 317–572–3985)
Fax: (U.S.) 800–569–0443 (Outside the U.S. 317–572–4002)

To order additional copies of this product or to browse other Pfeiffer products visit us online at www.pfeiffer.com.

To speak with someone in Product Technical Support, call 800–762–2974 or 317–572–3994 Monday through Friday 8:30 a.m. to 5 p.m. (EST). You can also contact Product Technical Support and get support information through our website at http://www.wiley.com/techsupport

Before calling or writing, please have the following information available:

- Type of operating system
- Any error messages displayed
- Complete description of the problem

It is best if you are sitting at your computer when making the call.

Pfeiffer Publications Guide

This guide is designed to familiarize you with the various types of Pfeiffer publications. The formats section describes the various types of products that we publish; the methodologies section describes the many different ways that content might be provided within a product. We also provide a list of the topic areas in which we publish.

FORMATS

In addition to its extensive book-publishing program, Pfeiffer offers content in an array of formats, from fieldbooks for the practitioner to complete, ready-to-use training packages that support group learning.

FIELDBOOK Designed to provide information and guidance to practitioners in the midst of action. Most fieldbooks are companions to another, sometimes earlier, work, from which its ideas are derived; the fieldbook makes practical what was theoretical in the original text. Fieldbooks can certainly be read from cover to cover. More likely, though, you'll find yourself bouncing around following a particular theme, or dipping in as the mood, and the situation, dictates.

HANDBOOK A contributed volume of work on a single topic, comprising an eclectic mix of ideas, case studies, and best practices sourced by practitioners and experts in the field.

An editor or team of editors usually is appointed to seek out contributors and to evaluate content for relevance to the topic. Think of a handbook not as a ready-to-eat meal, but as a cookbook of ingredients that enables you to create the most fitting experience for the occasion.

RESOURCE Materials designed to support group learning. They come in many forms: a complete, ready-to-use exercise (such as a game); a comprehensive resource on one topic (such as conflict management) containing a variety of methods and approaches; or a collection of like-minded activities (such as icebreakers) on multiple subjects and situations.

TRAINING PACKAGE An entire, ready-to-use learning program that focuses on a particular topic or skill. All packages comprise a guide for the facilitator/trainer and a workbook for the participants. Some packages are supported with additional media—such as video—or learning aids, instruments, or other devices to help participants understand concepts or practice and develop skills.

- *Facilitator/trainer's guide* Contains an introduction to the program, advice on how to organize and facilitate the learning event, and step-by-step instructor notes. The guide also contains copies of presentation materials—handouts, presentations, and overhead designs, for example—used in the program.

- *Participant's workbook* Contains exercises and reading materials that support the learning goal and serves as a valuable reference and support guide for participants in the weeks and months that follow the learning event. Typically, each participant will require his or her own workbook.

ELECTRONIC CD-ROMs and web-based products transform static Pfeiffer content into dynamic, interactive experiences. Designed to take advantage of the searchability, automation, and ease-of-use that technology provides, our e-products bring convenience and immediate accessibility to your workspace.

METHODOLOGIES

CASE STUDY A presentation, in narrative form, of an actual event that has occurred inside an organization. Case studies are not prescriptive, nor are they used to prove a point; they are designed to develop critical analysis and decision-making skills. A case study has a specific time frame, specifies a sequence of events, is narrative in structure, and contains a plot structure—an issue (what should be/have been done?). Use case studies when the goal is to enable participants to apply previously learned theories to the circumstances in the case, decide what is pertinent, identify the real issues, decide what should have been done, and develop a plan of action.

ENERGIZER A short activity that develops readiness for the next session or learning event. Energizers are most commonly used after a break or lunch to stimulate or refocus the group. Many involve some form of physical activity, so they are a useful way to counter post-lunch lethargy. Other uses include transitioning from one topic to another, where "mental" distancing is important.

EXPERIENTIAL LEARNING ACTIVITY (ELA) A facilitator-led intervention that moves participants through the learning cycle from experience to application (also known as a Structured Experience). ELAs are carefully thought-out designs in which there is a definite learning purpose and intended outcome. Each step—everything that participants do during the activity—facilitates the accomplishment of the stated goal. Each ELA includes complete instructions for facilitating the intervention and a clear statement of goals, suggested group size and timing, materials required, an explanation of the process, and, where appropriate, possible variations to the activity. (For more detail on Experiential Learning Activities, see the Introduction to the *Reference Guide to Handbooks and Annuals*, 1999 edition, Pfeiffer, San Francisco.)

GAME A group activity that has the purpose of fostering team sprit and togetherness in addition to the achievement of a pre-stated goal. Usually contrived—undertaking a desert expedition, for example—this type of learning method offers an engaging means for participants to demonstrate and practice business and interpersonal skills. Games are effective for team-building and personal development mainly because the goal is subordinate to the process—the means through which participants reach decisions, collaborate, communicate, and generate trust and understanding. Games often engage teams in "friendly" competition.

ICEBREAKER A (usually) short activity designed to help participants overcome initial anxiety in a training session and/or to acquaint the participants with one another. An icebreaker can be a fun activity or can be tied to specific topics or training goals. While a useful tool in itself, the icebreaker comes into its own in situations where tension or resistance exists within a group.

INSTRUMENT A device used to assess, appraise, evaluate, describe, classify, and summarize various aspects of human behavior. The term used to describe an instrument depends primarily on its format and purpose. These terms include survey, questionnaire, inventory, diagnostic, survey, and poll. Some uses of instruments include providing instrumental feedback to group members, studying here-and-now processes or functioning within a group, manipulating group composition, and evaluating outcomes of training and other interventions.

Instruments are popular in the training and HR field because, in general, more growth can occur if an individual is provided with a method for focusing specifically on his or her own behavior. Instruments also are used to obtain information that will serve as a basis for change and to assist in workforce planning efforts.

Paper-and-pencil tests still dominate the instrument landscape with a typical package comprising a facilitator's guide, which offers advice on administering the instrument and interpreting the collected data, and an initial set of instruments. Additional instruments are available separately. Pfeiffer, though, is investing heavily in e-instruments. Electronic instrumentation provides effortless distribution and, for larger groups particularly, offers advantages over paper-and-pencil tests in the time it takes to analyze data and provide feedback.

LECTURETTE A short talk that provides an explanation of a principle, model, or process that is pertinent to the participants' current learning needs. A lecturette is intended to establish a common language bond between the trainer and the participants by providing a mutual frame of reference. Use a lecturette as an introduction to a group activity or event, as an interjection during an event, or as a handout.

MODEL A graphic depiction of a system or process and the relationship among its elements. Models provide a frame of reference and something more tangible, and more easily remembered, than a verbal explanation. They also give participants something to "go on," enabling them to track their own progress as they experience the dynamics, processes, and relationships being depicted in the model.

ROLE PLAY A technique in which people assume a role in a situation/scenario: a customer service rep in an angry-customer exchange, for example. The way in which the role is approached is then discussed and feedback is offered. The role play is often repeated using a different approach and/or incorporating changes made based on feedback received. In other words, role playing is a spontaneous interaction involving realistic behavior under artificial (and safe) conditions.

SIMULATION A methodology for understanding the interrelationships among components of a system or process. Simulations differ from games in that they test or use a model that depicts or mirrors some aspect of reality in form, if not necessarily in content. Learning occurs by studying the effects of change on one or more factors of the model. Simulations are commonly used to test hypotheses about what happens in a system—often referred to as "what if?" analysis—or to examine best-case/worst-case scenarios.

THEORY A presentation of an idea from a conjectural perspective. Theories are useful because they encourage us to examine behavior and phenomena through a different lens.

TOPICS

The twin goals of providing effective and practical solutions for workforce training and organization development and meeting the educational needs of training and human resource professionals shape Pfeiffer's publishing program. Core topics include the following:

Leadership & Management

Communication & Presentation

Coaching & Mentoring

Training & Development

E-Learning

Teams & Collaboration

OD & Strategic Planning

Human Resources

Consulting